Song
of the
Phoenix

Song
of the
Phoenix

Voices of Comfort and Healing
from the Afterlife

Lily Fairchilde

St. Martin's Press 𝔐 *New York*

Design by Nancy Resnick

Library of Congress Cataloging-in-Publication Data

Fairchilde, Lily.
    Song of the phoenix : voices of comfort and healing from the afterlife / by Lily Fairchilde.
      p. cm.
    ISBN 0-312-15212-4
    1. Spiritualism—Case studies. 2. Spiritualism. 3. Fairchilde, Lily. 4. Future life—Miscellanea. I. Title.
    BF1261.2.F19   1997
    133.9'01'3—dc21   96-48914
                               CIP

First Edition: April 1997

10 9 8 7 6 5 4 3 2 1

to Sandy,
    who kept his promise
to Helen,
    for her boundless faith
to all of those courageous souls
    who shared their stories
to the angelic beings and guides
    who so freely shared their wisdom
to the Great Embodiment of Love
    known by many as Jesus
to Father Sky, Mother Earth, and
    all of my relations
and, most of all, to the Creator, to God,
    whom I thank with humbleness
    and deepest gratitude for the beauty
    of each day, for the beauty of this life,
    for the beauty of the Truth.

Contents

Acknowledgments

I would be remiss were I not to express my extreme gratitude to the people who believed, coaxed, supported, cajoled, and otherwise encouraged this book into existence. Without their expert and compassionate midwifery, it would have been an impossible task indeed.

So, here goes! Thanks to Helen Davis and her brother Sandy for being the catalysts who started the whole thing. Thanks also to Helen for all her support and encouragement. A big kiss and a great big hug to my family: to Billy and Brooke, and to my mom and dad, who never stopped believing, who exhibited the patience of saints during the months I was consumed by this project. Thanks to J.C. for a sympathetic ear and a great photograph! I am grateful to Norman Ratner for suggesting and facilitating a path that eventually led to the publication of this book. Thank you to Barbara Lowenstein and Eileen Cope, agents to die for. Thank you also to Charles Spicer, Stephen Murphy, and the brave folks at St. Martin's for taking a chance, for their understanding of a sometimes difficult subject, and for their editorial brilliance as great healers of manuscripts. Thanks also to Ray, Beverly, Skylar and Tim, Sandy and Garth, Becca, and last but not least, Ralph—soulmates if I have ever met any—for their love above and beyond the call of duty!

Author's Note

During the course of this book, I have used several terms to refer to the Ultimate Source of all life—God, the Creator, Great Spirit, the Divine. It is an impossible task to encompass this limitless, boundless energy in a word. The Ultimate Source is all-inclusive and, therefore, consists of both feminine and masculine attributes. These terms should be understood to include both the male and female aspects of the Divine. When it is necessary to include pronouns, the same truth applies.

When the term *man* is used to denote humanity as a whole, it is meant to include women as well as men. The truth is, we are all both male and female at the level of the spirit. The manifestation of both of these energies is necessary—in ourselves as well as in the whole—for the creation of balance and healing in the world.

Many of the souls you are about to meet speak of an afterlife encounter with a magnificent, blindingly bright being who imparts to them eternal bliss and peace. Several of these souls refer to this embodiment of Divine Love as Jesus. The identity of this Great Presence is understood according to the cultural experiences of each soul. The greatest of Divine Teachers has many faces and has appeared to all races and all cultures throughout time. The individual interpretations of each soul should not be taken as a religious pronouncement that limits, in any way, the truth to any one particular path. There is a yawning chasm between religion, which limits the experience of the Divine by way of exclusive definition, and spirituality, which encourages the free exploration of an individual's direct experience of the Divine without the need of intellectual scrutiny. All paths and all teachings that come from a loving heart open in surrender to God's wisdom have at their core the same message: Love is the way.

The events described in this book took place over a period of four months.

Introduction

As far back as I can remember, I have been aware of an otherworldly realm, filled with heavenly beings who loved me and were there for me constantly. They were my friends and teachers, comforters and counselors, playmates and helpers. They were with me at night when I slept and walked with me during the day. There was no barrier between hearts, such as the one I very quickly realized existed within most human interactions. They were more real to me than the people of flesh and blood who inhabited my material world.

I was continually surprised to find myself encased in a physical form in this rather rigid existence, ruled by laws that made very little sense to me. The first part of my life was spent coming to terms with the fact that my experience of reality was very different from that of most people.

I cannot remember a time when I was not aware of the emotions and true intent, no matter how well hidden, of those around me. I can immediately sense when someone is ill, or out of balance physically or emotionally. It is like I am a radio capable of receiving, as well as sending, a broader range of signals. I have never had a "spiritual teacher" or "spiritual training." My abilities are the result of a combination of genetic as well as soul factors in the equation of who I am this time around.

The way in which God has led me to express my essence has

nothing to do with personal power or Earthly recognition. The rather unique abilities I have been gifted with exist, not to make things difficult for me or to set me apart from the rest of the world, but rather to allow me to help in healing the imbalances in myself, in others, and in the environment. I have never advertised my services, and have declined any publicity or public recognition. It is not about parlor tricks. It is about healing and teaching and learning. It is about love given in humble service to those who ask with open hearts and minds. It is about surrendering myself so totally to the will of Great Spirit that I become a hollow reed through which the Breath of Life is given to others.

When asked to explain exactly what it is I do and how I do it, I am acutely reminded of how limiting definitions are. My work is fluid. It conforms to what is most needed at the moment by those who have come to me for help or guidance, for the healing of emotional or physical imbalances, for reassurance and empowerment. It is not I who decide what form this help or guidance takes, but rather a part of me that is far more wise and all-knowing than that part which has chosen to manifest in the world. Like all of us, my personality is the costume I have come to wear for this particular Earth walk. During my work, I temporarily discard the costume. It is too confining for the graceful, quicksilver movement of the Spirit.

At that moment there is no past, no future . . . there is only now. And in that now lie all possibilities, all realities. I am free to follow any possibility, to experience any reality. I have direct access to beings existing at these other levels, and they to me. I can witness a person's past, as well as the possible futures available to them, depending on which choices they make. Yet—and this is the most crucial point—I do not guide what I say or do in this space. Rather, I wait in the stillness for Great Spirit to convey to and through me the instruction and healing most needed by the one who has come to me.

Sometimes this takes the form of a sort of counseling session. We sit quietly together for a moment. If it is the first meeting between us, I take the time to ask what brought the person to me, and then explain what might happen. When I feel the person is comfortable, a brief prayer is said. With that prayer, I am no longer limited by the normal constraints of the personality. Yet this change does not dramatically affect how I present myself. My eyes do not roll back in my head, nor do I begin to speak in the voice of a two-thousand-year-old holy man!

What does take place is very ordinary in one sense. In another, it is a miracle—the miracle of a bonding of spirits in unity and one-ness, the miracle of a greatly expanded clarity, and with it the ability to truly know and experience another from a place other than ordinary mind. I am filled with a deep and holy love for the person sitting across from me. It is this love that creates the pathway through which any truth or healing comes. It is this love that opens the doorway to extrasensory perception, so that the presence of angels, spiritual teachers, and guides can make themselves known. I always feel them beside us, surrounding us with protection and comfort and love. Many times they can be sensed, even seen, by others in the room.

We all work as a team. The information I have access to in my expanded state is added to by my otherworldly helpers, who contribute their own unique viewpoints of the situation. Always they pour their great love and unbounded healing energy into and through us. This waterfall of light and clarity is infused into our bodies, minds, and hearts.

The seeker is then evaluated on a physical, emotional, and soul level, and given guidance as to how to improve his or her life, how to create the best possible future from the place where they are at present. Sometimes it is a shamanic journey that we take. This journey has very little to do with words, and everything to do with experience. We travel together, through the use of chanting and sound and the direct conveyance of energy to the seeker through me, to a place beyond ordinary mind, where inappropriate patterns can be revealed and shaken loose and reshaped into a thing of power and beauty. And always there is the great goodness and overwhelming uplifting presence of God and the angels, and a mighty ocean of ecstatic love.

Time and time again, I have been witness to the transforming power of this leap out of ordinary consciousness and its attendant limiting beliefs. Tasting, however briefly, the elixir of eternal life uplifts and rejuvenates those who are mired in confusion or suffering, those in despair over actions for which they feel they cannot be forgiven, those in the depths of grieving over the loss of a loved one, those facing their own mortality, those searching for true significance in a life that has lost all meaning.

During these sessions, we are sometimes visited by people who are no longer living. They may be relatives or friends, lovers, or even old enemies. They usually appear because there are unresolved issues that need to be addressed in order for healing to occur. They may have messages to impart. Possibly their death was sudden and they did not get to say their good-byes. Sometimes they come simply to reaffirm the eternal bond and everlasting love between souls, which will never die.

Whenever one of these disembodied spirits enters into our circle of expanded awareness, I experience a physical reaction. My electrical field is disturbed, my skin prickles, my heart races and pounds, I become very cold and temporarily disoriented. As this happens, I pull myself back to my center and adjust my level of perception so that I can serve as a communicator between those on either side of that invisible fence that separates the living and the dead.

It was one such session with Helen, a unique and lovely woman devastated by the loss of her beloved brother, which led to the creation of this book. The empowerment and healing that she gained from that meeting with her brother's spirit was overwhelming. With Helen's support and encouragement, I embarked upon an amazing series of experiences. I was visited by souls, once living like you and I, who shared their stories with me. These stories were conveyed in forms as simple and direct and real as these souls could make them, so that they could be understood by the majority of people. In life they faced differing challenges and played diverse roles. For some of them, the experience of death was beautiful and easy . . . a flight of freedom. For others, it was confusing and filled with fear. Yet ultimately their paths led them to a growing wisdom and a deeper knowing of themselves, and of God's loving universe. I have tried to the best of my ability to stay true to the vision they offered, to remain a faithful reporter—a sort of interviewer-participant in a strange yet, at the deepest level, very familiar territory.

I was introduced to Ruth, a beautiful young woman who took her life, along with that of her unborn child, when she despaired of living without the one she loved. Willow Dancing, a brave Native American girl, shared with me her death in the midst of violence and cruelty, and the vision of peace and unity she later found. I experienced along with Joey what the process of death is like for a child. I saw through the eyes of David what it is like to be a ghost. They, along with others, gave of themselves unconditionally, asking nothing in return, except that we listen to them with an open mind.

I had never before "channeled" spirits. *Channeling* is a phenomenon in which you turn your body over to another soul. That soul then uses your faculties to interact with this reality. Yet, as I listened to the stories of the spirits who came to help us understand this thing called death, presented with such trust and simple eloquence, I lost all sense of boundaries. As they shared with me their fears and joys, their suffering and their deliverance, I was drawn farther and farther into their realities, until their experiences became mine. I actually became them. I felt what they felt, spoke as they spoke, saw as they saw.

The entire experience is one that I will more than likely never repeat, nor shall I ever forget it. It was very hard on me physically as well as emotionally. As one-of-a-kind beings, we all have differing vibrational frequencies. These frequencies are as unique and as individual as fingerprints. Merging with frequencies foreign to my own familiar vibration created an imbalance in my physical body. I did not regain my normal physical integrity until this process was complete. In contrast to this experience, merging with the angels has never affected me adversely. It feels like home to me!

Angels contributed greatly to this book by giving us their perspective after each individual soul's story. These perspectives clarified and expanded upon what we had heard, and helped us to connect these stories with more universal truths pertaining to the experience of living and dying.

We all at some point question the meaning of life and death. Death—our own, as well as that of those whom we cherish—is something which we all will experience.

Think of this book, then, as your own personal journey into that profound, magical, yet very real land beyond death where angels and demons, saints, guardian spirits, and great holy teachers are not simply myths, but living entities. It is a place where all those who have been wrenched from you in death are forever living and loving you still. In this place all of your questions will finally be answered, limitation as we know it will be swept away, and true love and forgiveness and freedom will reign without end.

I am eternally grateful to those souls and angels who shared their stories and their wisdom with us, serving as our guides to a greater understanding of this mysterious journey we call death. I salute all of you who are willing to listen to these stories and this wisdom with an open mind and heart.

We cannot begin to live fully until we come to terms with the reality of death. We cannot know true courage until we look death in the face and see that it is not a voracious monster with yawning jaws that will eventually gobble up everything we hold precious, but instead a thing of beauty and wonder and great adventure. We will never be free to love fully and without fear until we know deep in our hearts the truth that love never dies, but lives on, along with those we have loved, forever.

All truth is, in the end, one Truth. The form that the truth takes in this book is only one way of looking at it. It is my deepest wish that what you read frees you from fear, that it empowers you and brings you peace, so that you may know the greatest love there is.

God Bless,
Lily

From the unreal
  lead us to the Real,
From darkness
  lead us to Light,
From death
  lead us to Immortality.

The Upanishads

There is but one freedom,
to put oneself right with Death.
After that
everything is possible. . . .

Albert Camus

Crazy Horse dreamed and
went into the world where
there is nothing but
the spirits of all things.
That is the real world
beyond this one.
And everything we see here
is something like a shadow
from that world.

Black Elk

Song
of the
Phoenix

1

Sandy's Story

I opened my eyes with a start. The clock by my bed read 3:30 A.M. The room, normally dimly lit by the night-light on my dresser, was now glowing with an unearthly illumination. The air was very cold and subtly vibrating. My body was electrified, my heart racing, all my senses alert. I had experienced these sensations enough to know what they meant—I was being visited by an otherworldly presence.

I had been awakened from a sound, dreamless sleep, and I was somewhat disoriented. I sat up in bed and centered myself with a prayer for protection and clarity. I became very still. My awareness moved from its normal parameters into a less limited realm.

By this time I knew that whoever this spirit was, it meant me no harm. Communication was its purpose. I slowed my mind until I could "hear" what this presence was so urgently attempting to convey. In this realm information is transferred in a telepathic manner rather than articulated by voice and heard by the ear.

Immediately I recognized this energy. It was Sandy, a client who had died of chronic heart disease a few nights before.

The last time I had seen him, several months earlier, he had looked worn and tired and much older than his sixty-odd years, his body ravaged by decades of health challenges. But now he appeared before me youthful, vigorous, and radiant.

"Hello, Sandy, what is it?"

"I want you to tell Helen that I am all right and very happy. Tell her that everything here is just marvelous. Let her know I love her and that we will never be truly separated. Please take care of her."

At this point my body was flooded by a tremendous wave of intense love. Tears sprang to my eyes. I was so emotionally overwhelmed at this point that I found it hard to breathe. As the illumination gradually faded away, the room temperature returned to normal. I was left, as I always am after these experiences, shaken yet with feelings of numinous wonder and peace.

The Helen that Sandy had spoken of is his sister, a lovely woman of great openness and sensitivity. The next morning I called her. I knew that Sandy and Helen were very close and had grown even closer following the recent deaths of their parents. Sandy's illness and subsequent passing had affected her greatly. I did not want to present her with information that she might not be prepared to handle.

I asked her how she was, and after listening for that sign between words that let me know she could cope with what I was about to tell her, I took a deep breath.

"Helen, I heard from Sandy last night. He came to see me and asked me to give you a message."

I gently relayed his words to her and did my best to convey the feelings of love and peace I had experienced.

She was delighted and greatly moved, but not very surprised.

"Before Sandy died, I asked him to contact me after he was gone, so I would know how he was and how things are where he is. Did he say anything else?"

I told her that I had given her the message exactly as it was given to me.

She then said, "Could I come over? Maybe Sandy would come and answer some questions for me. I have so many questions about what it is like there. I want to know what his experience of death was like. Do you think he would communicate with us?"

I told her I did not know, but was willing to try. I scheduled a meeting for later that week.

* * *

After settling ourselves in the chairs before the beveled-glass windows in the special room in my home reserved for my work, I began the prayer that precedes all of my sessions:

> *"Dear God, thank you for bringing us together in your Light and in your Love. At this time we are surrounded by the white Light of God, and with it the strength and the authority and the glory of God. Every cell in our being radiates the golden Christ Light, and with it the total perfection and absolute health of body, mind, and spirit; the love and the compassion, and the crystalline clarity of Jesus the Christ. We are surrounded and protected by God's love for us, and by our love for God. We are shielded from any inappropriateness. Open our hearts and minds and souls to Thee. We ask Father Sky and Mother Earth and all of our relations, and Great Spirit in whom we live and breathe and have our very being, to bless us and this endeavor. In the name of Jesus Christ, Son of the Living God, we ask these things; and in His Name, we know that they are done."*

This prayer was given to me many years ago by the angels who help me in my work. It reflects my grounding in the teachings of Jesus as well as those of the Native Americans. It is a statement of the reality that it is not I but the power of God which is responsible for any blessings, truths, or healings that are received during this time.

This prayer creates in me an openness and a conscious surrender to God's love and wisdom, and to the greater good of the whole. I consciously surrender my will to God's will.

I felt my consciousness move into a space of great stillness and peace. My body was totally relaxed and filled with love.

Helen asked, "Is Sandy here?"

When Helen spoke his name, Sandy appeared to my left smiling and glowing with well-being.

"Yes, and he looks radiant."

"Sandy, I am so glad you are here! Would you tell us what it is like where you are?" Helen quietly requested. "I really want to know what it was like for you to make your transition."

I listened intently, then replied, "He says he would be delighted to share his story with you. He wants you to know he is all right and how things are where he is. He will relay his thoughts to me, and I will put them into words and convey them to you."

After taking a few more moments to move deeper into that still place, I let Sandy know I was ready, and we began.

When I was in the hospital, even though I was in excruciating pain, I resisted letting go. You know how I love Christmas, Helen. I was trying to hang on for one more Christmas!

I was also afraid. Afraid that there wasn't anything more and that I would simply cease to exist. The thought of that unending nothingness terrified me. Even though I wanted so badly to believe in an afterlife, my literal mind kept getting in the way.

I am still unclear about all that went on around me during those last days. When my consciousness was centered in my body, things seemed very cloudy and dreamlike.

Many times I would slip out to my physical shell. The first time this happened I was very surprised! I found myself, suddenly and without warning, floating above my body. It took me a moment to realize that the person I saw in the bed below was actually me.

While I was in this out-of-body state, everything was crystal clear. I felt no pain, just very free and light. These intervals began to occur more frequently until, toward the end, I was spending very little time actually centered in my body.

This was really a wonderful way to prepare for my transition. I could get used to being out of the physical body without actually dying. The experience allowed me to let go of much of my fear because, for the first time, I realized that I could exist outside my body and that I was much more than that shell which, up until then, had encompassed the whole of my identity. The release of that fear made it much easier when I finally did let go of my life.

I spent much of this time floating around the hospital and hovering over my physical form. I was watching everything — operations in other parts of the building and procedures performed on my own body. Even though I knew it was my body, I did not feel the effects of anything done to it. It was as if I were observing the nurses and doctors working on a dear friend.

I visited you, Helen, when you came to the hospital, and once followed you out to your car! I grew accustomed to the mechanics of moving in and out of the body. I began to really trust this space and to much prefer it over the alternative of being confined to my physical shell, which was clouded with suffering, medication, and pain.

When I was out of my physical form, I noticed that my consciousness was contained in a body of sorts. It was much lighter and more mobile than the body I had grown used to, but I still had hands and feet — everything I was accustomed to having! This "light" body was attached to my corporeal body by a slender, glowing cord. Because of this connection, though I might not be in the direct vicinity of my physical being, if even the minutest change or threat to my survival were to occur I would be immediately aware of it and could then return to stabilize my body's condition.

I have learned that there are many people who are caught in a kind of limbo space — a place between your reality and the next — because they have not severed this cord and made the final disconnect from their bodies. There remains a very thin, ever-fading connection. As long as this connection is not consciously severed, their souls will not progress. That is why many people sense "ghosts" in and around cemeteries. This is a very sad and lonely existence — souls reluctant to let go of their bodies long after these bodies have ceased to be viable.

After several days of moving in and out of my physical form, from shadow to light and back again, I eagerly slipped from my body for another outing and I saw my parents in the corner of the room enveloped by a glowing halo of light. I was overjoyed to see them. The timing of their appearance could not have been more perfect. If they had come to me before this, I more than likely would not have trusted the reality of their presence. I would have told myself it was a dream or a hallucination. But by this time the experience of being out of my body had become more real than anything else. My former life and my physical shell were becoming very shadowy and unreal to me. I also was aware that the more time I spent out of my body, the lighter I was becoming. I see now that it was preparation, in a way, for a smooth ascent.

My parents asked me if I would like a glimpse of where I was going, and of course I said yes.

Immediately we were flying through a tunnel-like space at a tremendous rate of speed toward a brilliant light. As we entered that light, for the first time I could remember, I truly felt love. I know there were those in my life who loved me, but I only knew this intellectually. I could not *feel* it. On Earth, at this time, it seems that real love is the exception. Here it is all there is. It was overwhelming and beautiful beyond words. There were many others there, all radiating light, all filled with love — pure and unadulterated unconditional love.

I was then told that if I so chose I could "cross over." I had already assessed the true condition of my body. I realized that if I did go back I would live as an invalid. My actions and cognitive abilities would be seriously impaired due to severe damage incurred in the cellular structure of my brain. This was the result of oxygen deprivation caused by blockage of blood flow to that organ.

So I came back through the tunnel into my hospital room and into my poor, tired body one last time to say good-bye to it. I also wanted to check on you, Helen, to make certain you would be all right.

Then, I simply left. I slipped out of my body and severed that slender thread of life through a conscious act of will.

I have learned that sometimes, when one suffers a traumatic or instant death that is unexpected, this cord is severed as a result of the shock of the experience. The soul in its entirety shoots out of the body. These souls are given the option of reconnecting with their physical bodies if they so wish, and if the condition of those bodies allows for the continuation of life. This is the source of many near-death experiences. However, in instances where people are in comas or experience chronic lingering illnesses, this severing of the cord must be done through a conscious act of will.

We really do choose our time of death, you know. Many of the world's saints and holy men and women choose the time of their deaths with awareness. It is as if death is a river flowing by, and they choose when they will jump into it. They know when it will happen, and they make preparations for this momentous event in their soul's journey. In this way, their experience of death is smooth and clear — an ecstatic surrender.

So all of us, at some level, either consciously or unconsciously, do choose when we are to leave. This moment is not a calendar date that has been set from the time we are born. It is, rather, that there are certain situations and events we are to experience. Our souls choose that which we will accomplish and learn during our lives. When we have completed those tasks, then we are free to leave at any time. Some choose to leave right away, others choose to stay a while longer.

It is as if there is an A-list and a B-list of experiences. The A-list is made up of accomplishments that comprise our destiny. If we turn our backs on these, the spirit will remove us rather quickly from life. These experiences are the necessary next steps in the soul's progression. If we find ourselves in a situation, which for whatever reason, precludes the carrying out of our destiny, our spirit will choose to leave this life for circumstances that are more conducive to fulfilling our soul's purpose. The B-list is comprised of experiences which we would like to have, but which are not necessary for the completion of our destiny. This list is optional. Some people choose to complete both lists. Some simply grow tired after completing the A-list and decide to leave.

After I had separated my true self from my physical body, I was joined immediately by a great angelic being. He informed me that he was, in fact, my guardian angel! It was as if he were a part of me, yet not a part of me. Helen, I have never known such safety and total acceptance as I experienced in the presence of this being. I felt once again like a little child, trusting and totally secure with him.

I was given a choice: to cross over to the other side immediately or to spend three days in this space between the worlds, saying one last good-bye to the people and places I dearly love. I chose to say good-bye. I spent the next days making contact with all of those who are dear to me. I came to your apartment, Helen. Once, when you were at my house, I was able to get Casey [his cat] to notice me.

It was marvelous! I had simply to think of a person or a place, and I was there immediately. Really, it is more *feeling* a person or a place rather than thinking about them. I went once more to all the places that I so love — the Amazon jungle, the Arizona desert, the African veldt. Earth is so beautiful! I visited my daughters and my beloved. I spent much time with you, Helen.

The longer I was out of my body, the more difficult it became to maintain contact with your reality. I realize now that this was because my vibrational frequency was becoming gradually higher and therefore very different from that of the physical Earth.

Just before I left, I went to see Lily to fulfill the promise I had made to you, Helen. I wanted to give you a message and establish a link so that I could communicate with you. I had tried to reach you directly many times during the period following my death, but was unsuccessful.

After accomplishing this last task, I was ready to go. Immediately, I was joined by my guardian angel, and together we entered the tunnel. We began to move at great speed. I was moving faster and faster — it was not like walking but more like floating or flying. There is a very real sensation of movement, but it is different from any experience I ever had while in my physical body.

There was also a light within this tunnel, although it was nothing compared to the intensity of the light at the end. The light is perceived not only visually; you can feel it. It is a living essence. My body at this point was no longer what you would think of as solid. This light was able to pass through me, and it changed me. I began to feel lighter and lighter. All heaviness and any attachment to the reality I was leaving melted away. Vibrationally, I was being changed. Everything that could possibly prevent me from feeling love began to dissolve.

When I first left material reality and entered this tunnel, there was sound — there is always sound. The whole universe is made up of sound. This particular sound is overwhelming — a roar that moves from a very low to a very high pitch. It pulled me away and into the tunnel, and then suddenly ceased, and I was immersed in the indescribable harmony of Heaven. This celestial sound passed through my now changed body. I sensed it with my whole being, not just my ears. I heard it with my whole self.

When I reached the end of the tunnel, I was propelled forward with great force into a space of ineffable beauty and light. All of the colors here are incredible. There are hues that do not exist in your reality because they are a vibrational frequency above those that the human eye is able to perceive. These colors are not reflected off of the surface of things. They emanate as light from within each creation, so that everything appears translucent and glowing, rather than solid.

This place, which we call Heaven, contains the perfect pattern that God created for the planet, and all of the universes, and everything that ever was and is and shall be. From this archetype, the reality we know as Earth was formed. Every rose, every violet, every tree, every bird on Earth has its counterpart here in Heaven. If you can imagine the most beautiful, most perfect rose you have ever seen, then multiply that beauty and perfection ten thousand times; still it would fall far short of the spirit pattern from which that same rose was formed.

I have learned that the source of this dichotomy is the condition of man's consciousness. Mankind was made caretaker and co-creator of the Earth. We have chosen to build our world on beliefs in darkness, separation, and fear. We have created a reality that falls far short of God's magnificent vision for us. Because any whole can only rise as high as the vibrational frequency of the sum of its parts, all beings, all things in this reality are held back and prevented from manifesting their true potential on this material plane by the belief constructs contained in mass consciousness.

Almost immediately after I arrived, I was taken by my guardian to a beautiful temple-like space. The walls look like translucent marble, but are radiating light. There is a council there made up of twelve great beings. They are dressed in glowing robes, their bodies emanating light. These beings help to guide newly arrived souls through this transition period. They facilitate these souls' understanding of what is happening to them and the implications to their spiritual progress of the experiences they had while incarnated.

I did not feel any judgment or condemnation here, only compassion and acceptance, welcome and love. I was not afraid.

I was then told that it was time for a review of my life. I must explain that words are not the main method of communication here. I have learned just how limiting words can be. Instead, we merge our consciousness and transfer our thoughts as well as our emotions so that there is perfect clarity among us, with no room for misunderstanding.

The council explained that this was not a time for judgment, but a learning experience. They asked if I was ready. Then the most incredible thing happened. I reexperienced, in its entirety, the life I had just completed. Every little thing, even incidents which I did not remember with my conscious mind, came back to me. I relived the whole of my existence, only this time I saw it with a clear and understanding eye. I not only "saw" these events, I felt them. I learned the true impact of my actions by experiencing not only my emotions but the emotions of everyone I had interacted with. I was filled with pain, sorrow, and dismay over some of the choices I had made; pride and peace and fulfillment at others. One of the greatest regrets for me is that I gave fear so much power in my life. That fear was what prevented me from giving and receiving love. I felt much grief that I had not conveyed my true feelings to others. I mourned all the loving things I had not said. I saw that I had allowed fear to make of me a very self-centered individual.

I did not see this as a judgment — rather it was a revelation, which I experienced to the very core of my being. I saw how fear had limited me, and as I saw this I was healed, the pain and grief washed away. I do not know how long this review lasted — time as you know it does not exist here — but when it was done, I felt a peace and a completeness, and a total understanding and compassion for my life and the man that I was. This wisdom is now recorded on my soul and will be a part of me forever.

I was then led out of the temple and into beautiful gardens and forests of light stretching as far as the eye can see. Everything here is so vibrant and alive and sparkling.

There is always light here. This light cannot only be seen, but also felt as love. Its source is God. It fills everything there is. There is nowhere here where it is not. This light is so bright in Earth terms that were you to look upon it with the human eye, you would be blinded.

Helen, you would love it! Time and Space are very different here. Everything is happening at once. You simply move your focus from one thing to another to experience anything you wish. If you have a desire to create something, say a painting or music, you can just visualize it or hear it and it springs into existence immediately. And as your vision changes, those changes are instantly reflected in the new creation before you. Everything flows effortlessly from one form into another with ease and grace.

I saw many other souls walking and communing in the beautiful gardens, celebrating their existence along with the animals and birds. Some of these beings seemed to be made of the same essence as I. Some were angelic or devic spirits, who were larger and somewhat brighter and less dense in nature. The light that shines from them is almost impossible to describe in Earth terms. It is somewhat like a waterfall of brilliant, sparkling, pulsating energy.

There is much laughter and great joy here. I feel that everyone I see is a part of me. For the first time, I don't feel alone. Many souls came up to me and expressed their happiness at finding me here. Some, like my parents, I knew from my last life. Many were souls I had known in other lifetimes. We had long been on separate journeys and so had much to share.

The celebration of holy days on Earth is reflected here in Heaven. Anytime one being expresses love and thanksgiving on Earth, it is also felt and celebrated here.

There is no need for food at this level of existence. We are sustained by the great light of which we are so inextricably a part. I am told that human evolution is moving rapidly to a place where you, too, will live on light.

Helen, I have seen Jesus. He truly is God's son, a perfect embodiment of the Holy of Holies. The love that He is instantly transforms any sadness, doubt, or fear. He can be in all realities at once. He is boundless. He has no limits. He is here to help us remove our own limitations and rise in love. He has appeared in many forms, to all cultures, in all realities throughout existence.

There is no disease here. The bodies we have are light bodies. They are very fluid. Although we can merge with and experience anything imaginable, we do not become attached to the experience or out of balance as the result of it. Instead, it flows right through us like ripples on water.

There is a time here when every soul chooses what is next for it. There are infinite choices. Will you reincarnate on planet Earth? Will you spend time serving as a guide for someone still in a body? Will you spend more time here learning in the Heaven realm? Will you journey to other realities? I have not decided yet what my next step will be.

One thing I do want to do here is to help the animals and the environment of the Earth. There is much grieving among many on this side over the effects of man's actions on the planet.

The space you call Heaven is really everywhere, intermingled with your space, only at a different frequency. Same space — different frequency. All space is one. That is why everything you do in your reality affects everything in every other reality. That is why everything we do here affects you there in the same way. There are so many prayers on both sides for the healing of Earth and all of her creatures. The grieving is being turned into powerful prayers. We see your prayers as brilliant beams of light reaching into the universe. We link our prayers with yours and in this way the consciousness of man is changed. You must not give up hope!

Finally, I must tell you about the libraries here. They are magnificent temple-like structures. These structures are translucent and glowing. They are not filled with books, but with light and what I can only term the complete and total awareness of all things. Many of your temples and holy places on Earth are modeled after these heavenly edifices.

If you are curious about something — someone or some event in history, for instance — you enter into a temple, and by simply thinking the question you immediately receive the answer. This answer comes not only as an intellectual concept — it is visceral. You see it, feel it — you become it. All things that every individualized spirit has ever experienced from the beginning, all possible realities that ever have or ever could exist are recorded here. You can reexperience and in that way know anything. All the wisdom, all the knowledge, all that ever was or is or shall be is contained within this light.

"What about the horrors?" Helen asked softly.

They, too, are recorded here, along with a total understanding of what caused them, and what their implications are for the evolution of the individual soul as well as for mankind as a whole. In reexperiencing one of these so-called horrors, it is possible to gain a clearer understanding of why it happened. You are able to see into the very hearts of all of those involved. You become these individuals to gain compassion for them and clarity about their actions.

This can be a very important experience for those souls who

have not been able to forgive certain incidents, whether they be personal or historical. It is imperative that they come to a place of forgiveness. Without forgiveness, it is impossible to rise in love because that lack of forgiveness for one of God's creations means you are rejecting a part of God. There can never be total love without total forgiveness. This does not mean you must accept as appropriate the atrocities that are troubling you. Rather, it is that you do not reject the soul who through ignorance, pain, or fear perpetrated that action.

In this way, even the most horrendous act can be used to the advantage of the whole by providing a powerful experience through which to learn and grow.

Many times, when souls are preparing to incarnate, they come to these temples to learn the histories of the families they are to be born into. They can learn directly about their fathers or their mothers, their sisters or their brothers — even the life histories of their great-great-great grandparents are available to them here.

If they choose to come incarnate with the gift of music, they can relive the lives of Mozart or Beethoven. They can become that person in these learning temples, and in this way acquire the soul knowledge of these gifted individuals to help them complete a chosen life destiny.

This is why, sometimes in your reality, people who are, for whatever reason, not in accord with the truth of their own being will become confused and believe that they are Cleopatra or Napoleon or Leonardo da Vinci. The accumulated knowledge of these historical figures was imprinted on their soul in a learning temple and carried into material reality to be recalled if needed to assist them in their true life path. Instead, they confused it with their own individual soul's history.

The temples are one of my favorite experiences here. They are sometimes referred to as the "Akashic records"* on Earth.

Helen, there is so much more I wish I could describe to you,

---

*The Akashic records, or universal mind, are where all possibilities, all knowledge of past, present, and future, are held.

but there are truly no words in the human tongue to communicate them. Just know that it is wonderful and wildly ecstatic beyond your greatest dreams!

"Is there anything else?" I asked Sandy.

"Just that I want Helen to remember how beautiful she is and that I love her very much."

"Thank you, Sandy. Good-bye for now. I love you, too," Helen replied.

As she said these parting words to Sandy, I felt my own energy begin to coalesce once more, becoming centered in this time and place.

I then said the closing prayer:

> *"Dear God, thank you for this great love and wisdom, which You give and we receive with much gratefulness. As we go forth from this day forward with the courage to follow the path set before our feet and the strength to be who we really are, we shall see with the Eye of God, hear with the Ear of God, know with the Mind of God, speak with the Voice of God, and love with the Heart of God. I thank you for making this so. We thank Father Sky and Mother Earth and all of our relations, and Great Spirit in whom we live and breathe and have our very being, for blessing us and this endeavor. In the name of Jesus Christ, Son of the Living God, we have asked these things, and in His name we know that they are done. Amen."*

This prayer completed the circle and expressed my gratefulness for the help we had received.

Many of the concepts Sandy had related were not new to me. I had encountered some of these things myself in two near-death experiences I had over a decade ago and in the numerous out-of-body episodes that have occurred throughout my life. And I had received much of this information in other forms during the many individual sessions and workshops I have given over the years. Still, the impact of these truths never loses its power and transcendence for me.

This session with Helen and Sandy was the beginning of a powerful journey of exploration into the depths of these truths. What followed was a series of encounters with other souls who have made the leap from this life into the next, with mighty angels, with spirit guides and teachers. Helen was with me at some of these meetings. At others, I was alone. All added their unique perspectives to create an exciting and miraculous vision of death and its ultimate meaning to us in our evolution as spiritual beings.

2

Devas, Saints, Angels, and Spirit Guides

*A*ll of the souls I spoke with talked of angels—ethereal helpers who are there for them to offer love and comfort and guidance. They also described meetings with deceased loved ones and with beings of sparkling light filled with great wisdom and power.

God-like entities appear in the mythologies and religious histories of all cultures—mystical beings possessing abilities that far exceed any capabilities recognized in the average human. Gods and Goddesses, saints, angels, devas, otherworldly guides—their existence holds an ancient mystery, which has the power to lift us out of our narrowed focus on what is possible, what is real.

There is but One God, the source of all creation, all-inclusive, all-knowing. This Divine Essence has many aspects and contains within the whole all of the perfected, balanced higher emotions and qualities of enlightenment. There are great beings, god- and goddess-like archetypal entities that exist in the realm of the Spirit, which are made up of the purified, distilled essence of Divine Qualities. Holy Father, Holy Mother, Holy Child, Warrior, Nurturer, Lover, Healer, Creator, Compassionate Judge, Wise Teacher—these are but a few aspects of the evolved whole that have taken on an individualized essence in order to bring the qualities embodied in these ideated forms nearer to the vibrational frequency of the human form. These Shining Beings serve to slow down the vibrational frequency of the Divine so that it may be more directly accessible to humans without causing harm to the physical body. This is necessary, for the origination point of this frequency is so far beyond the normal range of human existence that, were you to access it directly in your present state, the molecular structure of your corporeal body would literally be blown apart.

Archetypal entities serve as reminders of what we can be, of those aspects that we ourselves hold and have access to—available in the deepest recesses of every soul. They can be called up and embodied within our personalities when we align our energies with those of the Creator.

These God-like beings have been known by many names. They appear to us in dreams, in waking visions, at times of great emotional distress or ecstasy, during personal or planetary crisis. They offer to us wisdom, inspiration, and a transcendent awareness. When confronted by their majesty, we are lifted out of the confines of our linear reality into a timeless space. We are given the opportunity to merge with these superhuman strengths and qualities of understanding and unconditional love so that we may accomplish the task at hand in a clearer and more balanced way.

Although there is a part of their essence present in every spirit, these entities also possess distinct physical forms which exist at a vibrational frequency far above that of our reality. At one time, they were able to walk among us, for the frequency of our reality had not slowed to the point at which we now find ourselves. Because of the choices we made as a collective consciousness, this frequency was lowered—so much so that the present human level is not compatible with the high, finer vibrations of these great heavenly spirits.

As we begin to make different choices—ones that create balance and harmony, unity, lightness and love on the planet—then the frequency of this reality will return to a level where these god-like beings will once again be able to walk among us. Until then, they remain as close to us as the air we breathe, watching our progress, inspiring us, and providing us with Divine examples of the true strengths and eternal qualities of the spirit.

Whenever a human in his life-walk has as his focus the development and strengthening of one of these Divine aspects within his soul, then these great beings draw near to that human to offer guidance. If that soul surrenders totally in its heart, mind, and spirit to the manifestation of this godly aspect, that soul then becomes a human embodiment of this Divine Essence on Earth.

Many of these gifted humans become recognized as saints—those who in their life have surrendered their will, their whole existence totally to the will of God and to the Divine Plan, which has at its very foundation the good of the whole. They become so selflessly immersed in the Love and Compassion and Wisdom of the Divine—so devoted to realizing the Creator's perfect order within their souls and in promoting that order and truth in the world around them—that they transcend all patterns of separateness. They are then consciously one with the whole of Creation, one with the Creator. They become living conduits of pure love and wisdom and courage and compassion, manifesting these attributes through their human form, serving as a Divine inspiration and example to those still struggling toward that final complete surrender to the will of God.

Many of these fully realized souls, when they leave their corporeal existence, choose to continue to serve the good of the whole by remaining close to this reality, always ready to respond to prayers for help and healing and guidance offered up by those with a clear and sincere intent.

Saints serve as holy counselors, ever responsive to the pleas of humanity. Because many of them suffered terribly in life, they understand intimately the cries of a soul in pain and confusion, despair and need. In their compassion, they allow the energy and emotion of those soulful petitions to be magnified through them. These prayers are then answered by the Creator, the suffering one comforted by these holy saints who were once human, who walked the Earth, who experienced great pain yet transcended that pain to reach a state of enlightenment.

Rather than being victimized, their souls weakened by their adversities, they instead—by choosing to respond to these experiences as warriors in spirit, with love, compassion, faith, and great courage—became transfigured and freed from the overwhelming pain at the heart of all suffering: the illusion that we are separate one from another, separate from God. Saints bring healing solutions from the Divine to those who ask with an open and humble heart. They will continue to serve in this capacity until humans, by their actions, shake off the bonds of illusion that separate them from God's wisdom, Grace, and great transformative Love.

Angelic beings are also present at all levels of reality to offer help and guidance to those who ask. Their existence is inextricably interwoven with that of human souls, although they are not of the same vibrational frequency. Their path of learning, of evolution as spirits, is also different from the human path.

Angels carry a higher, finer vibrational frequency than do humans and are less dense in nature, more light filled. They, as a consequence, have realized a more fluid existence. They are able to easily move between worlds and to take on different forms when needed. Their natural reality is pure balance and does not contain the extreme polarities that fuel growth and generation at this Earthly level of evolution. They are, therefore, naturally androgenous, although they can polarize their energy in order to create a male or a female form when this is called for. They are aware at all times of their oneness with the Creator. They never lose sight of this oneness. They are the pure and radiant embodiment of this Sacred Truth. They serve as God's messengers, as reminders of this Truth for all of Creation. They are caretakers in the soul garden of the Divine, lovingly tending their charges, ever-watchful protectors of humans and animals—of all sentient beings in God's Cosmos.

Angels have many times appeared to those in distress to rescue them, to guide them through a crisis. They materialize in human form by temporarily slowing down their vibrational frequency. When the crisis has passed and they are no longer needed, they literally seem to disappear, retreating to their natural state of invisible watchfulness by then raising their level of vibration. Once in a great while, an angelic spirit will incarnate into the world—being born, living, and dying as a human. During this angelic visitation, the lives of all will be changed through their interaction with this otherworldly being in human flesh—the vibration of Earth, of man's consciousness as a whole heightened by this enlightened presence.

You each have a guardian angel who accompanies you to this

world when you are born. They are there for you when you die, to comfort and encourage you and offer you unending, transformative, unconditional love. They never leave you. During your Earth walk they can be called on to add their strength to yours, their courage to yours, their compassion and understanding to yours—to carry you over the rough spots in the road. However, they will not do this unless they hear a plea from the soul for assistance, for they are bound to honor the universal law of free will. They will not interfere with the ability of humans to make their own choices. They do hear every sincere call for help, and if that request is in alignment with the soul's destiny—the completion of which is, in the heart of every soul, its deepest desire—they will then offer to that soul Divine intervention and sustenance.

Angels are eternal, beautiful, filled with light. They have always been there for you from the beginning of time. Their singular purpose is to serve God, to serve those souls who wish to merge their wills with that of the Divine and thus make their journeys back to the One.

There are also souls, human in nature, who serve as guides and helpers to those still living. These disembodied spirits are a part of the embodied human's soul group—that group of souls who travel together through incarnation after incarnation, serving as teachers for one another, learning the same lessons, balancing the same imbalances, sharing similar destinies, similar vibrational frequencies. Some of the souls in a group may choose not to incarnate during a particular period, serving instead as guides, as guardians for those who have chosen to inhabit a physical body. Too, when a soul leaves the Earth before the rest of its soul family, that soul will often stay close to this reality until all in its family have finished that particular incarnation. This family is one that is related not necessarily by blood but by intent.

The souls serving as guardians choose to continue their growth and evolution by offering assistance and guidance to keep the embodied souls focused on the completion of their particular destiny. They communicate—as do the angelic messengers—through intuitive knowings, through dreams, through the manifestation of external signs, whose meanings are unmistakable to the intended receivers if they have the faith to trust what they see and hear. By then having the courage to act upon this information, their lives are inevitably changed and enhanced for the better.

Many times a member of our soul group will accompany our spirits to this Earth plane along with our angelic guardians. They are present at our birth, and they will be there upon our death to help us through our resistance and fear, to remind us to keep our eyes and hearts ever turned toward God, and to join with us in glad rejoicing at our homecoming. Angels and saints, spirit guides and Gods' great Divine representatives—although for the most part invisible to the human eye—are accessible to the heart of us all. In truth, even when it seems we are alone and without hope, we are instead surrounded by a host of otherworldly beings. They will always be there—eternally loving us through all the rough spots on the way to our final, most joyous destination.

3

Ann

*H*ow does a soul become a spirit guide? During my counseling sessions, I often hear from these heavenly helpers. They are usually relatives or loved ones, long deceased yet still near to the living, come to offer guidance and comfort. Why do these spirits choose to stay close to us, rather than going on to experience the wonders that await them? Ann's story offers insight into one reason a soul might adopt this path of service.

She came to me on a day when the whole world seemed filled with a golden brightness. After enjoying a walk in a nearby arroyo with my dog, Peaches, I perched momentarily in the lap of a great rounded stone to drink in the beauty of the high desert. It was then that I sensed a change in the energy surrounding me. I closed my eyes, and when I opened them again, I saw a great distortion of the air, as if I were looking at things through a watery screen. It was Ann, come to show me her life, her death, and the wisdom she gained from these experiences. I relived it all with her. There on that warm solid rock, I experienced all her emotions as she had experienced them. I saw through her eyes. When it was over, I returned home and wrote down all that I had heard and seen.

My name is Ann. Dying wasn't easy for me. I fought it from the second the physician found the lump. I fought it through all the operations and the dashed hopes and the realization of my worst fears. I fought it until the end, through the pain and the rage and the helplessness and the tears, until I had nothing left to fight with. It was only then that I began to understand. It was that moment of stillness which allowed me to see the truth.

The truth is, I had begun to die long before the cancer showed its face. It is an inner death I speak of, a death of the heart, a numbing of the soul.

I had always thought of myself as a woman of courage, a survivor. Now I see that what I took for courage was really cowardice born of the fear of being abandoned, as I was by my parents who were too busy to remember a small, timid girl. This girl needed them more than they would ever know, yet she was shuffled from one caregiver to another, until the day she was able to fend for herself. I was given everything money could buy, everything but the love that would have healed my deep and abiding fear of the world. Because of this fear, I built an impenetrable wall between myself and my feelings. I took pride in being totally self-sufficient, in not needing anyone.

There was no one on Earth who could penetrate this barrier . . . not my husband, not my daughter. I was a powerhouse in the world of business. I had nothing but contempt for anyone who showed the slightest sign of neediness, weakness, or softness. Compassion was to me an idealistic concept, but one that did not translate in the real world. In that world, if you did not cover your back, someone would surely shoot you down at their earliest convenience. Compassion was a luxury I did not believe I could afford. It angered me when I saw it in my husband. It frightened me when I saw it in my child.

My life was ruled by the law of accumulation . . . accumulation of money, material possessions, power, recognition, success. No matter how much I had, it was never enough. Acquisition was my first priority. Yet this carried with it a high price. I drove my husband, Theo, away, alienated my daughter, Leslie, and in the end I lost my life.

But these losses held for me a great discovery. As I was

lying helpless in that hospital bed in those last days, I discovered love . . . something I had stopped believing in long ago. Despite my rejection of its existence as anything other than fantasy, love had indeed been there inside me all along. I had simply been afraid to let it out. Now all my defenses were ripped away, and love was loosed by the sight of my daughter's face. As I stared into Leslie's eyes through a haze of drugged pain, my heart suddenly opened like a flower, releasing a torrent of impassioned love.

I was swept by this great wave of love into the past. I remembered the day that my little girl—she must have been three or four at the time—had run up to me, her face beaming like the sun, her eyes bright with innocence, a bouquet of red and blue petunias she had pulled from my garden extended in her pudgy hands.

"Here, Mommy!" she had chimed, her voice filled with shy pride. She threw herself into me, her soft warm body smelling of new grass and sweet earth. And what did I do? I pushed her away, scolding her for ruining my garden and wrinkling my skirt. The sting of those thoughtless, harsh words was as deadly as if I had slapped her with all my strength. She had literally reeled with the hurt, staggering away to fall on her little backside. The memory of the look of pain and betrayal in that precious tiny face, wet with tears, welled up from the deepest recesses of that dark place inside where I had never before allowed myself to go.

I remembered too the time she brought a picture home from school. She had labored long and hard over that painting . . . a masterpiece of childish wisdom that she had labeled "My Family." Her father had displayed it proudly on the refrigerator. She had been so excited for me to see it, but my only comment as I rushed in late, as usual, was, "Take that down, would you? It doesn't really go with the decor, now does it?"

Theo's face had darkened, thunderclouds of disapproval obscuring his normally cheerful expression. Leslie had quietly removed the once treasured, now offensive picture, crumpled it up, and thrown it in the garbage.

"I'm sorry, Mommy," she had whispered before running from the room. She had actually said *she* was sorry, when it was I who should have begged her forgiveness.

A few years later, when she was just starting college, her father left. She blamed me for that, and rightly so. I never had time for him. I was too busy impressing the world with how successful I was. Leslie began to spend more and more time with Theo and his new wife. I hardly noticed.

Then I got sick, and this made me run even harder. When Leslie married, my only concern was making sure everyone we knew was impressed by the size and elegance and tastefulness with which I orchestrated the wedding. Whether Leslie was happy or not was of secondary importance to me. It was shortly after this that my physical condition began to deteriorate rapidly, and in a matter of months, I had run out of time.

As I looked deep into my daughter's eyes in that final instant, I knew that it was too late. God, I would have given anything, thrown away all that I had gained in the material world, for just one chance to show her how much I loved her — had always loved her. It was a love so deep and rich . . . how could I have denied it? How could I have been so cruel — to her, and to myself?

I tried to say the words . . . to say, "I love you more than life," but my lips were growing numb. Tears were streaming down my face. Howling winds of despair and grief wracked my body with a pain much, much worse than any I had experienced during my illness. A strangled cry of horror at the irreversible momentum of my leaving and the irrevocable damage I had done by my thoughtlessness leaped from my convulsed soul.

The next awareness I had was looking down at myself in the hospital bed. My daughter was frantically calling the nurses, who rushed in with the doctor following close behind.

"I love you, Mommy . . . I love you, Mom. Please don't go . . . Please don't leave me! Please, Mom . . . Oh, God, please . . . no!" The wailing of my daughter drowned out the screaming alarms of the machines with their flashing lights.

I was dead. That was the message those steel sentinels were broadcasting to the world. But I didn't feel dead. Physically I felt better than I had in a long time.

This was totally unexpected. I had been raised by a family whose religion taught that there was basically no survival as a separate consciousness after death; that the only rewards were those gained during your life; that you lived on through your children and your children's children. So how, then, could this be happening?

Though I felt very different, I was still aware of myself as an individual. I could still feel the overwhelming despair that came from realizing — too late — that I had thrown away the only truly important thing life has to offer . . . the chance to give and to receive love.

I was desperate to comfort my sweet, incomparable daughter. She looked so vulnerable, so devastated. Why was it that now when I finally saw how much she needed me and how precious that need was, I was unable to comfort her, to hold her and make it better? I became frantic, distraught. I moved closer to her, trying to give her something — I don't know what — that would ease her suffering. But it was no use. She could not hear me. She could not see me. Her cries seared my soul.

"God, if you are there, help me, please!" I cried out with every fiber of my being. "Please, don't let her suffer like this!"

Suddenly, I felt a hand on my shoulder. All of my anxiety drained away. I turned to see who was with me, and was shocked to discover a beautiful young man, radiant with light, standing close by my side.

"She will be all right," he said, "and so will you."

"Who are you?" I whispered.

"I am what you would call an angel. I have been with you for a long time, and I am not going to desert you now." He smiled. "Come with me."

"But, I can't leave my little girl!" I was sobbing at this point, tears of grief mingled with tears of joy. Tears of grief at knowing I would never be able to go back to my daughter, would never get the chance to make things right for her. Tears of joy and relief at being in the presence of someone who I knew loved me and would care for me.

My angel could read my thoughts. He knew everything I was feeling. "Come with me," he repeated gently, "and you will see how you can help her. There is a way."

He held out his hand, and with a final backward glance at what had been my life, I let him lead me away. Immediately the room, my daughter, my lifeless body all vanished. I was engulfed in a blinding, bright light. This light wrapped around me like a blanket and I was carried like a baby into a new world.

Waves of love and peace washed over me. I journeyed with my angel through a place of pulsing, healing light and sound until suddenly all movement stopped, and I found myself in a space filled with a golden radiance. I could feel the presence of a mighty goodness, although I could see nothing but the light.

I knew that this presence was ultimate Love and endless Compassion. I was asked if I were willing to submit without resistance to something which, although it surely would be difficult, could ultimately free me and make me whole.

I learned then what true courage is. It is the willingness to look at your life clearly and to accept responsibility for your actions. It is staying open to love despite the pain and fear of this self-examination. I had never before hurt so deeply. To see the suffering I had caused others was like having my innermost being shredded by a thousand jagged-edged swords. The torture seemed never-ending. Yet, by the end, I had also seen the hurt I had endured as a young girl, which had contributed to my actions. And although this did not excuse my choices as an adult, it allowed me to see clearly the truth of things. With clarity came compassion. This Divine gift of compassion allowed me to forgive myself, as well as those who had hurt me as a child.

Forgiving myself, I was now ready to accept my lessons, integrate them, and move on. Yet there still remained a deep desire to reconnect with my daughter, to help her in some way. I longed with all my heart to bring balance to her life, to heal the imbalance I had caused. No sooner had I formed this desire than my angel appeared before me in the golden light, which is more than light—it is a Living Presence.

"There is a way for you to help your daughter. She is soon to become a mother. The soul who will be born to her could use a guide to help her along her life path. This way of service is open to you . . . a means of expressing your love for your daughter by caring for her family. This is something you must choose for yourself; we cannot make this decision for you. It is not an easy way. However, it is a way that holds much learning and joy and completion—for both you and your daughter, as well as for the young one soon to be born."

"But I don't know how to do this! How can I be a guide for another, when I myself have so much to learn?"

He smiled. "Can you love this soul?" A young woman with eyes of light and a smile of tender mercy appeared beside him. "If you can love her, then you can guide her with the wisdom of your heart."

This beautiful vision reached out to me and instantly became a part of me forever. "I am Eleanor," she said, her voice filled with music. "Your daughter and I have been together before. I love her so much, and will be with her again very soon. But when I enter into human form, I will forget much of what I know to be the truth. I will need someone to be there, someone to speak to me in my dreams, someone to remind me of what is real, someone to help me when I have lost my way. I would like it very much if that someone were you."

How could I refuse such an eloquent plea? And so it was that I left the golden light and accompanied this exquisite soul to Earth, and was present at her birth in the same hospital where I had taken my leave in such pain and despair.

The room was filled with the rejoicing song of angels as Eleanor became my daughter's pink, sweet firstborn child. She had been moving in and out of the baby's body as it had taken form in Leslie's womb, traveling back and forth between heaven and Earth. Now, the totality of her bright, shining spirit infused the perfect new little being lying there on her mother's belly. The sacredness of that moment lit up the entire universe — the holy union of spirit and matter.

Little Eleanor turned her head and looked straight at me, standing beside Leslie, my hand resting on her head. "I thought for a minute I saw my mom," Leslie said to her husband, who was beaming with pride and love.

I have been with Eleanor, watching her grow, learning from her experiences, learning from my service, and in this way healing the imbalance in my soul. Because Eleanor and I have formed a union of spirits, even though she has consciously forgotten our heavenly agreement, she feels me near her as a comforting presence. I communicate with her through a bonding of hearts. She senses my warnings or guidance, should she need them, as a bodily sensation of caution, as an overwhelming need to change direction, or to follow a certain path, no matter how irrational it may seem.

And my daughter . . . I see my daughter's strength. I see her ability to turn old wounds into the wisdom that makes her the nurturing, affectionate mother I could not be for her. I have so much to give her, so much to say. I know that one day, when it is her turn to cross over, I will have the chance to pour into her all my love, to share with her all that she has taught me, and to ask for her forgiveness.

As for Eleanor, I was with her before her birth; I will be with her when she leaves her body to reenter Heaven. Birth is a door between worlds, as is death. Both are sacred, and to be honored. Both are a Divine celebration of the immutable, unchanging Love of God, and the everlasting light of the Spirit, which is forever moving, yet never far from the Source of all Life.

Remember to live your life to the fullest. Treasure each and every moment, for these moments in their uniqueness will never come again. Loving is the truest success. I pray that I will never again forget this.

* * *

Our angelic teachers want us to know that: "The ability to express love to those still living does not end with the death of the body. There are many ways to serve God, many ways to grow in spirit. The path that Ann has chosen—to stay close to the Earth, helping others in her soul group, and learning from that service—is one way. It is a path of great heart and immense courage."

4

Developing Awareness

*W*e all have unseen guardians who watch over us with loving attention. Some of them are people we related to closely before their deaths. They can even be ancestors whom we never met in this life, but who are connected to us by an indestructible bonding of souls. And there are always our angels, constant yet unseen companions.

How do we know when these otherworldly helpers are near? How can we communicate with them? How do they communicate with us? How can we know if the spirit we perceive has our best interests at heart, is trying to help rather than hurt us?

It is simple to establish communication with those loving spirits and angels. They are always aware of every thought, of every emotion that you send to them. This is true whether you accept the reality of their existence or not. The great challenge for most of us is developing the awareness necessary to receive and accept the information they constantly are giving us.

Communication of all kinds comes to us through the five senses: sight, sound, smell, touch, taste. Messages move from the outside world of our physical reality through one or more senses to the inner realm of the mind. There these sensations are interpreted according to our understanding of reality. We may also receive information in more subtle ways: through intuition, instantaneous knowing that can, without any apparent cause, well up from deep within us to register on and be interpreted by our consciousness.

Information from other worlds can be received in both ways. However, because we are dealing with a higher, more subtle energy than that of our physical reality, these messages are often obscured by the denser, and therefore more overwhelming, information we are constantly bombarded with in this society.

Communication with other realms most often occurs through the second, more intuitive method: spirit reaching deep inside us, by-passing the overloaded mind to tug at our hearts, leaving a lasting imprint on our souls. These messages are then translated into a conscious knowing. This is called *clair-sentience.* Usually this information registers as a strong emotion, which comes suddenly for no apparent reason. Deep feelings of comforting safety, ecstatic joy, immense love, or overwhelming fear can convey reassurance, union, passionate care, or warnings from our ever-present helpers.

Sometimes these messages are accompanied by more direct physical manifestations. For example, whenever one particular angel is around me, the room is filled with the scent of night-blooming jasmine. If your mother was fond of roses, you may smell the delicate essence of these special blossoms, announcing her presence.

Some people actually hear their name being called by the familiar voice of one long gone. Or they are surrounded by beautiful, unearthly singing, or the ringing of bells, letting them know they are not alone. They may hear a clear voice telling them to "turn around" if they are approaching a dangerous situation. This is known as *clair-audience.*

Once, I was heading blithely down the interstate on a cross-country trip, radio blasting, singing at the top of my lungs, when I distinctly heard a gentle yet commanding voice order me to "get off at the next exit." I had just stopped for gas, so my tank was full. The car was running smoothly. I could see no apparent reason for this command, but I had learned long before this how imperative it is to heed these messages, even if they seem to make no sense at all. So, I obediently pulled off at the next available exit and into a gas station. I visited the ladies' room, then walked around, idly looking at the fascinating geegaws you usually find nowhere else but at the gas stations and truckstops of Middle America. Finally, after replenishing my supply of bottled water, I headed out the door to resume my trip, none the wiser as to the reason for the urgent message I had received.

"Ma'am, is that your car?"

I turned to see a rather dashing young man pointing in the direction of my up-to-then trusty steed. I nodded in the affirmative.

"You've got a pretty bad flat there. You need help fixing it?"

Well, of course I did, considering I had removed my spare before leaving home in order to have more trunk space. He accompanied me over to inspect the sick tire, which by now resembled a flat black pancake wrapped around the axle. He determined that I had a slow leak that could be fixed "right across the street there."

I looked up, and sure enough, painted in large, faded red letters across an old gray building were the words TIRE REPAIR.

"You're a lucky lady," he drawled. "A few miles farther, and you'd a been in the middle of nowhere!"

In no time, the ancient but wonderful mechanic who belonged to the red sign had fixed my tire, charged me twenty-five dollars, and I was once again on my way. I spent the next hour expressing my deep felt gratitude for the care shown to me by the young man, the old mechanic, and last but not least, my constant unseen companions.

Visions may be utilized to convey to you something you need to know. I have many times been the recipient of these picture messages, showing me what is out of balance in the person I am attempting to help. Invariably, the visions prove to be accurate. This means of perception is known as *clairvoyance*.

Sometimes guardians will take on a physical form, appearing before you in order to help or to deliver a message. Recently, during the ongoing drought in Arizona, an elderly Navajo woman and her grown daughter, living in an isolated desert dwelling, received one of these miraculous visits. The mother, who could not speak as the result of a stroke she had suffered, said to her incredulous daughter, "Someone is coming."

Before the daughter had time to recover from the shock of hearing the clear voice of her until-then-mute mother, there was a knock at the door. She opened it to reveal two very tall, slender men; divine emissaries of the Holy People, the creators and spirit guardians of the Navajo. They said they had come to deliver a message to the elderly woman, who was to then carry it to her people. The message was that the people had become lax in their spirit ways. The Holy People wanted to help them to heal the land, to heal their situation, but were unable to because the ancient spirit ways were not being kept. They urged a return to honoring the Earth, to prayer and respect for the Beauty Way, the path of harmony with all of creation. If the people did this, the spirit guardians would once again be able to help; if this was not done, they warned, the people would not survive.

Their message delivered, they turned and walked a few steps and then vanished before the astonished eyes of the woman and her daughter. All that remained were two pairs of very large footprints, which ended abruptly, and a heavy sprinkling of corn pollen, always present when there is holy interaction with the spirit guardians of the Hopi and Navajo peoples.

The mother and daughter took their message to the elders of their tribe, who then delivered it to the people. Soon there was a pilgrimage to the now sacred sight where the two guardians of the people appeared. This incident sparked a revival of the spirit ways. It rekindled hope in the hearts of these people who still rely on the land to support them and are fighting valiantly to hold on to a vanishing way of life—a tradition filled with wisdom that has allowed them to survive all manner of hardships. The Native American cultures of the Southwest are some of the few that have retained knowledge of how to work with the forces of nature. If they continue to nurture their ancient ways, they will survive, even if the rest of the world as we know it self-destructs.

I was in Flagstaff, Arizona, with a friend during the time of this holy visitation. We had just attended an exhibition of renditions by native artists of kachinas, spirit beings who teach and nurture and help to give form and meaning to the universe. We were sitting beneath a beautiful old ponderosa pine, talking about the sacredness of these holy guardians of the people. We then began to discuss the pain and suffering we felt in the Earth. The land was so thirsty, and so very sad. In order to discover if there was anything we could do to help, we became very still, opening ourselves beneath that great old tree to a place beyond the ordinary world.

There, I was visited by one of these spirit beings, who told me that the Earth in that area was experiencing a great imbalance because we, as her guardians, had abused her, ignoring her needs. They said that this made them very sad. They wanted to help, were ready to help, but they needed the people to go back to their holy ways. They said that the practice of these ways had become in most cases a hollow performance.

They showed me that, in the old days, the priests who served the various kachinas during ceremony would live a life of demanding ritual, dedicating themselves from an early age to the practices that allowed their bodies to become appropriate vessels for the manifestation through them of these holy otherworldly beings. The continuous observance of this life of service allowed the vibrational level of these priests to reach a point at which they could merge with the finer, higher world of the kachinas, actually becoming them for the duration of the ritual.

According to what I was being told, the old ones who understood these things and still practiced them were almost gone. The young people were more interested in the ways of man's world, lured by alcohol, television, and the cities away from their connection with the land and the people. There was no one willing to do what was needed, no one willing to make the personal sacrifices necessary to offer themselves as a connection between Earth and the world of Spirit. Until the people changed their ways, they could do little to help. Without a human counterpart, it is difficult for them to manifest in our world for any length of time. Dedicated priests offer a door through which they can interact directly with the people, helping them to maintain balance in their lives, balance in the Earth. The priests carry this otherworldly energy in their bodies and their souls, inspiring the people, reminding them of their true nature, of their true place in the universe. Without those doors, the kachinas must remain in their world, waiting to be asked for help with the appropriate intent.

Pray, they said. These prayers would help the people to open their eyes, to remember what is really important, to resist the pull of a false world, to return to the old ways that had nurtured and sustained them from the beginning of time, since they were given life.

I relayed this information to my friend, and we spent a few minutes opening our hearts in love and respect for these beautiful spirit beings, for the native peoples, and for the patient Earth, who has given and given to her children, only to be ignored in her suffering, in her need. Two days later, as we were leaving to return to Santa Fe, we bought a local newspaper. It was then that we learned of the appearance of the spirit beings to the Navajo women, and the message they brought, which was so similar to the one we had been given.

The more sensitized you are, the easier it becomes to perceive and to understand these heavenly messages. We are continually receiving guidance and reassurance and love from this unseen world, yet most of us fail to acknowledge what we are being given.

This failure stems from two things: fear of the unknown and the numbing that comes from living in a society focused almost entirely on things material. We feed the physical, the external, yet starve the spirit. This creates a deadening of the senses and higher emotions, which, in turn, inhibits our ability to perceive. Most of us lead such busy lives that we never take the time to be silent, to listen to our hearts, to hear the voice of our soul. When we are presented with alone time, we fill it up with television, telephone calls, newspapers, the Internet—you name it! Anything to avoid the introspection that silence inevitably brings. Our spirits are imprisoned in mass-consciousness with all of its built-in limitations, and although we may from time to time entertain the notion of a reality that exists beyond the one we have grown accustomed to, it remains just that— an intellectual notion.

In order for us to directly experience the truth of this expanded understanding of how the universe works, we must first increase our sensitivity. For example, contact with this other world often comes when we are faced with a crisis—when we lose someone to death, during times of extreme stress, grave illness, or serious danger. The sensitization of certain neural receptors at these times comes as a survival response: the more information available to us at these times, the better our chances of surviving them. Experiences of transcendent joy and love can also increase this sensitivity by stimulating the release of certain hormones, which in turn allows the brain to receive a broader range of information, to experience emotions more intensely.

You do not necessarily have to be in grief, in danger, or madly in love to develop these abilities. You can gain greater sensitivity by adopting a life-style less involved in the man-made world and more open to the world of Great Spirit.

Experiment! Take two weeks. During that two weeks, abstain from reading the paper, turning on the radio, watching television. If you choose to listen to music, let it be unstructured and soothing to the soul. Put away your computer. Don't pick up the phone unless it is absolutely necessary. You might want to schedule this to coincide with vacation time and forewarn those who are close to you that you will be unavailable during this period. If you do not live alone you should definitely obtain the cooperation of your family or your roommates.

Spend as much time in nature as possible. Devote at least an hour each day to doing nothing. Really open your eyes, all of your senses, to the world around you. Breathe deeply. Eat consciously, lightly, abstaining from all animal products, alcohol, unnecessary drugs, sugar. Eat as much fresh fruit and vegetables as you can. What you do eat, take in with an awareness that what you are ingesting has a consciousness of a sort, and that it is giving its energy so that you may have life. Practice feeling the Spirit in everything around you. Sleep alone, if possible. Within these two weeks, you will begin to sense more, to feel more, to know more. You may like this so much that you will make what started out as an experiment a way of life!

Greater sensitivity, when it is balanced by a centered life, gives you the power of an awareness possessed by few. Yet, along with this must come a caution: walking in a world as imbalanced as ours can be at times excruciating in such a sensitive state. There is much pain, much suffering on our planet at this time. This is why we as a society are running so hard: it is so we do not have to acknowledge this harsh fact. Yet only when we are willing to feel it will we take this great imbalance seriously. It is then that we will find within us the power to make the changes that are necessary if we are to heal as a people, and as a planet.

Because of this increase in sensitivity, many things that you could do before may now seem difficult, if not impossible. Large cities may feel like giant whirlwinds of chaotic energy, psychic war zones to be approached with awareness and great caution. In a room with angry or distressed people, you could feel as if you are being physically assaulted. Your empathy level (your ability to feel what another is feeling) increases to the point that, until you learn to reestablish your boundaries in this new expanded state, you may not be able to discern what part of your emotions are legitimately yours and what part is originating elsewhere.

A sensitized body, mind, and spirit weakens the belief in separation, so that you are then able to feel the truth of oneness with all that is. It becomes a reality for you rather than an intellectual concept. And with this new reality comes a greater ability to experience things not of this world. There are many things out there in other realms, most of them wonderful and loving and kind. Some are not so wonderful. There are troubled souls and their thought forms. They are desperate for contact, for acknowledgment of any kind.

Evil is real; it is not an appropriate energy to open yourself to. Therefore, if you choose to increase your sensitivity, you must also beef up your armor. You can do this by cultivating the practice of daily prayer and meditation. This will enforce your conscious connection with God, thus keeping your intent clear and your body, mind, and soul balanced, strong, and aware.

If you do this, you will know immediately—sometimes beforehand—when someone approaches you (whether in a body or out) whose energy does not promote balance and well-being. You will receive a warning in the form of a physical sensation: a feeling of increased weight in the air around you, a pressure at your solar plexis—rather like the feeling you get after a narrowly missed accident. You may experience dread or bone-chilling cold.

Evil has the capacity to present itself in many forms in this other realm, some of them outwardly very beautiful. Your mind may be fooled by this charade, but if you listen to your heart, to that part of you that is forever directly connected to God, you will never be fooled.

If you ever find yourself in a face-off with evil, or you are presented with a lost soul who would be better served by turning to their guardian angel for guidance and help, rather than attempting to manipulate you in some way, center yourself immediately. Then, with the power given to you by Great Spirit, which resides always in your deepest heart, lovingly but firmly command the inappropriate energy to leave you and your surroundings and return to its appropriate space. Ask the help of God and the angels in this.

Your body will always feel fear in the presence of evil. That fear is there to warn you of something that would be foolish to ignore, something that could threaten your continued well-being. Yet you are much more than your body; much, much stronger than the fear. Call upon the great Love that you are, which connects you with the whole of Creation in all its glory. The Love of the entire universe is then at your disposal. Nothing is more powerful than that Love. Your body is the exclusive domain of your soul during your incarnation. No disembodied spirit can harm you unless, because of misplaced pity or need, or a surrender to your fear, you allow it access. Always remember that by cultivating love in your life, you are nurturing the truest strength there is. Love is the ultimate protection of everything that matters. In the end, it is the only protection.

Angelic wisdom

*A*t every session the angels immediately made themselves known. They are beautiful, incandescent, radiant beings filled with a great power, and, at the same time, a tender gentleness. They are much different from the way we are. Their presence, though awe inspiring and overwhelming, is never threatening. Rather they feel like home, like peace, like safety. They feel like love. I always feel them before I see them. I am lifted up and surrounded by their presence. It is like being in a room with your very best friends. You know they know everything there is to know about you and they love you anyway. There is never a question of abandonment or judgment . . . only unconditional love and joy.

To the eye, angels appear to be ageless. Their form is much like ours, only their light is not hidden or dense, but shines forth in a radiant halo. This halo surrounds them and consists of many colors that we cannot normally perceive with our physical eyes. There is always an abundance of gold and blue and pink and silvery white, in addition to the heavenly hues. This cloak of leaping, living light radiates outward and can appear at times to take the shape of wings. If need be, angels can slow down this dance of light so that they appear more human, more like us, less shiny. At that point they can be seen by a greater number of people. They will do this if there is a special need.

Whenever angelic beings were encountered an intense energy filled the room. I was swept up by rhythmic waves of power and peace and carried to a place of great stillness. I was freed from the confines of mass-consciousness, freed to accept and understand the universal truths that would then be so readily offered. I would lose all sense of personal identity, while still retaining an awareness of my individuality. And, as always, afterward those present were left greatly enriched and expanded by our experience of this Divine expression of truth and love.

We are messengers of God. We love you immensely, unconditionally, and without end. We are serving as a conduit for these truths in the hope that they will set you free to love and be loved, free to experience the limitlessness of your beings as well as that of the universe which awaits your acknowledgment.

We do not exist in some faraway nebulous Heaven World. In many ways, we are a part of you. We are not separate from you *or* from God. There is no place where you are that we are not. We are simply focusing and expressing our consciousness, our souls, at a higher vibrational level.

To demonstrate the fact that beings as seemingly separate as angels and men are indivisible parts of a Divine whole, the angels used as an example the creation of a rainbow from a single ray of light as it passes through a prism. They reminded us that although the red ray appears to be separate from the violet ray, the green ray from the blue, this uniqueness is actually a product of the differing vibrational frequencies contained within the light as a whole.

"So it is," they said, "with the whole of God's Creation, and the many levels of reality, the many ways of expressing one's existence as an individual soul. All seemingly different, yet all connected to form one perfect, brilliant, sparkling ray of God's Love."

Our heavenly teachers also pointed out that light contains rays that we are unable to perceive with the human eye; nevertheless that part of reality in which heavenly beings exist is just as real as what we can see, and equally as important.

* * *

Part of our task is to make available, to make more accessible and understood, those frequencies, those levels, that seem to be invisible, and therefore less real to you than the one in which you presently find yourselves.

The accepted means of communication in your reality at this time is the spoken word. Language arises from and is processed through the linear mind. Therefore, we will attempt to translate these truths into a linear form. Because of this somewhat limited mode of expression, these concepts will not be as complete as we would wish. Despite this limitation, the information will be delivered in such a way that what your mind cannot grasp through words, your heart will hear and understand.

The angels told us they would be giving us as detailed a picture as possible of these truths. We would then be called on to use the understanding of our hearts and a knowing that exists beyond the mind to grasp the Divine concepts in their entirety. This process is somewhat like viewing an abstract painting of, say, a woman in love. Although the rendering of this subject by the painter may not depict the woman in a manner to which we are accustomed, it nevertheless eloquently expresses depths that a portrait limited to a more literal interpretation seldom can. Yet if we were to focus on the form only, we would miss the emotion and true meaning conveyed by the combination of form and color and their relationship to each other on the canvas—by the dynamics created through the synergy of all these elements, as well as by that indefinable something that only the soul can see.

They reiterated that "every soul who hears these words will recognize the totality of their truth and fill in the parts which cannot be expressed in written language."

These beautiful beings then went on to explain the difference between the "spirit" and the "soul" of a man.

The spirit is not confined by linear space and time. It is never separated from the source of all creation and is, therefore, forever perfect and pure and whole—at one with God. The soul is that part of the spirit that takes on an individualized form. This form is *seemingly* separate from the whole.

That soul is given free will to create what it wishes of its existence. It may choose to turn its back on God and His Divine Plan and wander far, down dark and twisted paths, and lose its way. However, even in that journey there can be an enrichment of the whole. Each experience of darkness and pain and isolation will eventually lead back to the light. God uses every experience to his own end. That end is to create within every individual soul greater and greater longing for union, greater and greater capacity to love. In this way, every spirit is enhanced. In this way, too, God is able to create and love and grow and change. For as we change and grow, so does God.

The idea that God is affected—is actually *changed*—by our actions, by how we react to our experiences, by what we become, is an astounding concept to many. To help us understand the truth of this more fully, we were told that souls are to God much as individual cells are to the physical body. And that, although the body of man is changed as he experiences life, as he expresses his creativity and grows to maturity, the innate spiritual essence of that man remains the same.

So it is with the maturation process of the individualized parts of the Divine. Each soul is an individual cell within the body of God, infused with His Spirit, born of His Love, held close in His Heart. Therefore, our growth and expanding wisdom cannot but affect the form of the Divine Creator. This Holy Essence is ever-changing, yet the same.

The angels constantly stress the importance of cultivating flexibility and an openess of mind and heart at this crucial time of such great and rapid change on our planet.

It is most important that those of you who are immersed in the limited beliefs that form your modern cultures accept the sacredness and mystery of the cycle of death and rebirth. You must accept the fluidity of your being. You must let go of rigidity and stagnation and resistance to change. It is of utmost importance that all of those concepts that engender fear within the individual soul be released. They are formed of ignorance. They will be dispelled by acceptance of the Truth.

This truth—that although change is the essence of our deepest nature, we can never be separated from the Source of all Life and Love, we can never truly die—is the key to manifesting our highest potential in the days to come.

"Your reality is experiencing metamorphic events at an increasingly rapid rate—the birth pangs of a new way of being. Many will face the transition known as death—leaving one reality to enter into the next. Some will realize a transformation of the very form through which this transition is experienced.

We believe that death is a process in which our bodies, for whatever reason, are no longer able to function in a manner which can sustain life. Some of us feel that this is the point at which we cease to exist. Period. End of story. Some believe that the soul is separate from the body, and that when the body "dies," the soul moves on to another realm. Very few of us have ever considered, much less accepted as a sane alternative to these commonly held beliefs, the idea that we could be so transformed by the growth of the soul and this opening to Love that we will be taking our bodies with us when we go—an experience spoken of as ascension. Yet, the angels are telling us that this is exactly what we are moving toward in our evolution!

The belief that the spirit of man is separate not only from the material world but from the body as well helped create the process which you know as death. There is another way to experience this transition—a way that is in alignment with God's original plan for you. In this perfected transformative experience, not only the spirit and soul, but the body as well, is lifted to higher and higher frequencies until your entire being merges with the Heaven World in a brilliant flash of light and an intense ecstasy.

Until that time, it is important for you to accept that life *is* change. Stasis is the real death. Transition is necessary to the life and well-being of the spirit. You must allow these truths to penetrate to the very core of your being. The burning light of this wisdom will melt away the fear and contraction that limit you. You will then be able to experience your transition with joy and openness rather than with panic, terror, or denial.

These contracted emotions, along with self-judgment, are what hold the soul back and keep it trapped in the space between worlds. They blind you to the truth and create a false reality. This illusion is then projected onto your actual experience, so that the truth of what is occurring is hidden from you.

In other words, it is our belief system—our inability to embrace change without fear, our inability to accept our immortality and our inalienable right to unending unconditional Divine Love—that prevents us from experiencing fully who and what we really are at every level of existence. The angels want us to know that:

However it is experienced, what you call death is simply a passage from one reality to another. It is a time of intensity and wonder and change. A time to let go of one way of being and embrace another.

Every soul comes to your reality with an inner knowing of the truth of this limitless, endless adventure as an inseparable part of creation. All souls carry a memory of the glory of other realms. For a short time after souls are born into your world, they live with an awareness of these other levels of existence, and they speak with angels until they learn the language of man. It is at this time that the linear mind becomes dominant in most individuals, and they choose to shut the door on the wonders they have known. However, these truths are still held within the genetic pattern of every human. When they are ready and they choose of their own free will to open the door, these truths and this wonder will once again be theirs.

The information we relay to you can be a key to that door — a reminder of what each one of you knows in your deepest heart. Yet, because one of God's greatest gifts to you is free will, there may be those who choose not to accept with their minds what their hearts cannot help but hear. And, in the end, this too is as it should be.

If you could see the whole, you would see birth into your world as the real death and death as the real birth. Yet both experiences are necessary. Each world holds gifts that you cannot receive from the other. All of these experiences, these gifts, are needed for the rounding off and smoothing out of the jagged edges of the soul. These jagged edges — the rough spots — were formed during the journey out from the One. They are smoothed and polished clean by the journey back, until the soul becomes a perfect, reflective, brilliant orb of pure radiance and love.

6

The Story of Willow Dancing

On an overcast morning, as I sat watching a pair of bluebirds dance their celebration of spring, I became aware of a presence beside me. This unseen spirit felt very familiar, and somehow feminine. She stayed with me all day, and that night, as I was preparing for bed, she made herself known to me. I had just finished my evening prayer and meditation. When I opened my eyes, there before me stood the most beautiful Native American girl. As I listened to her story, I became her. She feels like a sister to me. The experiences she shared with me that night became my experiences. Today, I feel as if she walks with me still. She has become an indelible part of me. Perhaps she has always been with me, in a way. I have a deep and abiding love for this woman with a great brave heart.

I have had many names, but in the life I tell you about I was called Willow Dancing. This is because, even as a child, I was slender and moved with grace, as the willow moves when it dances with the wind.

I lived as a Cheyenne. Life was sweet and life was bitter in that time, the time of the vanishing buffalo, the time of the white man's rage. The fire of that rage ate up all that was precious to the People — the land of our ancestors, the freedom to walk that land as we chose, the trees, the buffalo, and finally our very lives.

As a child, I knew nothing of this sadness. I knew only the dance of the long golden grasses and the safety of my mother's lodge. I spent many days following the buffalo with my people, many nights by the fire talking to the bears which my mother had painted on our lodge skins — for my father was a man of great medicine. It was then that I learned of the story belt. It was then that I began to record the things that happened to me on a fine piece of elk skin that my cousin gave to me from his first hunt. The beads were beautiful and spoke to me in the symbols of our people, which came to life in this belt as I grew.

In my seventh winter I found my pony, my greatest friend. I saw her drinking from the spring, standing alone. She did not run from me. She was not afraid, and so followed a few paces behind when I returned to camp. Father said she was a gift from Great Spirit. We found a feather from the tail of a red hawk tangled in her mane. This was a most sacred thing. I named her Wears a Feather. It was not long before she welcomed me on her back.

Wears a Feather carried me through many, many moons. She carried me as I became a woman. She carried me in my wedding dress of the finest white buckskin to meet my husband, Three Elk. She carried me to the sacred mountain to pray for a son.

She had the heart of a great warrior, and she died as a warrior in my eighteenth summer, taking a bullet from the enemy's gun that should have taken me. I lived that day to tell of this thing with a bead in my story belt — the belt, which among all my possessions I held most sacred, for it told the story of my people, the story of my life.

It was not long after this that I followed Wears a Feather into the Spirit World.

It happened like this. We had spent many days traveling to a place which you know as Sand Creek. There, other people had gathered — mostly Cheyenne and Sioux. The camp was filled with women and children and with the old ones who had not yet lain down to die. My husband rode into the camp with me. Great Spirit had not called him away from his Earth walk as He had so many of our young braves. Three Elk took this as a sign that he had been spared to care for those who could not care for themselves. He and two others from another tribe left the same evening at dusk to find the hiding places of the enemy. We had not seen them but we could all feel them near, like a great killing storm of fire and ice.

As I watched my husband ride away, his back straight and proud, a great fear came over me, but I could not let myself think of what this might mean. Instead, I busied myself with helping those with young ones. My prayers for a child of my own had not yet been answered, and now I was glad of this. I would not have wanted my child to have suffered in the way that many of our little ones had.

Our people were weary and hungry and weak, but our spirits were still strong and unbroken. Yet we carried mourning with us like a sickness in our bellies that ate at our hearts day after day. That night I saw this mourning looking out at me from the eyes of the People as I helped them carry water and comfort their children and cover their old ones with what blankets they had left to them.

I went to sleep filled with the tears of my people and a longing for the safe return of my husband.

I was awakened by a scream of terror. Within seconds it seemed the whole of creation was screaming. I stumbled out of the lodge and into a nightmare. All was confusion and madness and running and red blood and red flames and death — everywhere, death for my people. No one was spared — not the old ones, not the sick, not even the babes in their cradle boards who hid their faces in their mothers' streaming hair as they ran from the enemy, ran from death.

But death was everywhere that day, and when it found me it wore the face of a blue-coat with yellow hair and eyes filled with madness. I saw a young mother I had helped the night before. The enemy had violated her, then taken her life as she lay facedown in the soft grass. Her girl child was stumbling away toward the water, and as this blue-coat with the yellow hair reached for her laughing, I ran to her, thinking somehow to shield her from this ugliness, this terror.

It was then that the madness possessed me, and I fought this white-faced bad spirit with the strength of all my ancestors. But in the end I was no match for his long, shining knife, and as I watched my blood flow like a bright red river from my belly into my mother the Earth, I knew my time with her was ended. I sank to my knees and lay my head where I could see the sky. Then I whispered the death chant and waited as the pain left me and the cries of the dying faded away.

It was then that I saw the shining spirits of our ancestors. They were walking calmly and with grace among my people who had fallen, gathering their spirits, comforting them with a welcoming song, and helping to prepare them for the journey away from this Earth home and to the lodge of Great Spirit who lives beyond the stars.

My grandmother was there for me in her brightness. She held her hand out to me and pulled me away from the body that had housed my spirit. She then clothed me in my wedding dress and placed my story belt around my waist. These things had been lost to me in that time of sorrow and destruction for our people. But everything of beauty that is created in love and prayerfulness has a life in the spirit world, and so the song that my spirit sang through these things was not lost, but was given back to me filled with life and glowing with an inner light.

I was now ready for my last journey as Willow Dancing. All that I knew — my body, the yellow-green grasses, the trees, the rushing waters, the lodges — even the cries of my people — were swallowed up in a great flash of light. And then I heard the thundering wings of the mighty Spirit Bird. This great being of fire and light swept me up and then we were moving faster than the fastest wind. We entered the darkness of the sacred mountain, and as I was carried through the heart of this mountain and into the Spirit World I could feel others of my people near. So many had ended their Earth walk in that time

of flowing blood, of flowing tears. And so it was in a river of
Spirits that I made my journey. I could see only darkness and
light. I could hear only the song of the Thunderbird's wings
and his powerful cries, but I knew that my people were there
with me.

Then in a flash of brilliant light we left the sacred mountain
and the Thunderbird set me down in the Land of Great Spirit.
I could now see, but it was with new eyes. And what my eyes
saw my heart embraced with great joy! For there was Wears
a Feather. Three Elk was with her for he had met death shortly
after leaving camp that night of the blue-coats. Together we
walked toward the Great Council Fire, accompanied by the
loving spirits of our ancestors who welcomed us with much
celebration.

There were twelve Great Spirits around this Holy Fire,
which lit up all of Creation. Three Elk and I left Wears a
Feather with our ancestors and entered the circle from the east.
I then lost sight of my husband but I could still feel him close.
My eyes were filled with the light of the Sacred Fire, with the
light coming from these Great Spirits. They wore bodies of red
and black and yellow and white, but the same light shone
within them all. Their spirits spoke to mine and I knew that I
was home.

Then from the heart of the fire rose two great beings. They
were made of this fire, which is the heart of Great Spirit. As
they walked toward my place in the circle, I could see that
they were Sweet Medicine and White Buffalo Woman. These
two had been sent by Great Spirit to our people to bring us
wisdom and to teach us many things. And as I looked into
their eyes I knew that they saw me and understood what I did
not have the words to speak. My heart was full and in its
fullness I was changed.

And then in the fire I saw my life as Willow Dancing. In
that Great Light all things were made clear and whole and
new. All the pain and anger and hatred of our white brothers
that had come to walk with me when I saw what they did to

the People, when I saw what they did to the Earth in their ignorance — all was burned away and in their place wisdom and forgiveness and, above all else, love now stood tall and strong in my spirit.

When I finally left my place in the circle, I knew that my path had been good. It had led me here to where all that I love lives forever. Wears a Feather runs strong and free with many horses, their bodies sleek and light. There are buffalo as far as the eye can see, moving like a brown river through glowing golden grasses. Deer run swift as the wind, their tails flashing white as they leap with joy. And the Great Eagle and Mighty Hawk dance in the sky above me, all perfect and whole and made of light — the Light of Great Spirit. In my walk with Mother Earth, I felt this spirit around me many times, but that knowing was as a small coal glowing in the deep night compared to this light that I now know.

And as much as our hearts danced together before, the love that Three Elk and I celebrate now is even more beautiful and clear. We are truly one — with each other and with all the people.

I am learning much here. There is only One Clan, and that is the Clan of the People — white, black, yellow, red — we are all one. Sweet Medicine taught us that. The fear of those who are different is what destroyed the life of beauty that my people once knew. It is one of the greatest enemies that you face on your Earth walk. Learn to move with courage through your fears into the wisdom of this union of spirits. Honor your differences — they are the gifts that you have brought to share — but do not ever forget that your hearts are one. In this way Great Spirit will be honored. In this way, too, Mother Earth will be served, for in this way your eyes — which have been blinded by fear — will be opened to a great truth. And that truth is that you all share one mother — the Earth — and that your mother is dying.

Would you not do what you could to save your mother? If you and your brother had bad blood between you and your mother needed you, would you not heal the hurts between you to unite your hearts to help your mother? This is as it should be. This is the truth of the spirit. This is the way it is here, in the Home of Great Spirit beyond the sacred mountain, beyond the stars.

7

Angelic Perspectives on Transition and the Afterlife Experience

The story of Willow Dancing told of a Heaven World and an afterlife experience that were very different from Sandy's, although there were some commonalities. During a follow-up session, the angels shared with Helen and me their views on the reasons for these seeming differences, as well as other information on the realms that exist beyond the world of the living. The map to these other realities became more decipherable for us.

There is one Heaven World, but there are many levels, many expressions of that world. For, in truth, everything meets in one space. One space, simply differing vibrational levels *within* that same space.

There are never-ending levels of awareness beyond the one at which you find yourselves, consisting of finer and finer gradations of light. There are spaces beyond your immediate Heaven World which we cannot convey in words or visions, for they are very foreign to your understanding of reality.

With each transition comes a different set of experiences. You cannot know the dynamics of the space in which you find yourselves until you fully know and experience the space immediately below it. Yet, you carry an awareness of these limitless levels of existence within your spirits.

The heaven-space which is spoken of in your so-called myths and legends is the vibrational frequency that holds the archetypal pattern of your world. It is the reality that you experience upon leaving the world in which you now find yourselves. It is the frequency through which you must pass on your way to higher and higher frequencies, to greater and greater soul expansion and wisdom and love.

Each soul will move between your world and this heaven-space until it has reached a level of understanding and love that will allow it to pass gracefully and with ease into the next level of experience. This process is that which you term *reincarnation*.

The exact nature of the transition and afterlife experience varies with each individual culture and with the belief constructs of those cultures. The way a person lives while in your world—their mythology and understanding of the workings of the universe—determines the form their transition will take.

However, every soul's transition holds similar characteristics. The essence of all life—all truth—is the same, yet how these experiences appear is a function of the individual soul's level of understanding. The truth is filtered through each individual's idea of how things work. Nevertheless, there is only One Source, one gift of life and love—ever changing yet everlasting. The same gift for every soul presented in different boxes . . . the size and shape and color of these boxes determined by each individual soul's experience.

Each soul, from no matter what culture or religious background, will experience the tunnel and unearthly music and living sounds that affect them profoundly. They each experience the brilliant light of Heaven and otherworldly beings—both familiar and unfamiliar to them. They each will experience a review of their most recent life. They all encounter that Great Being, the perfected Child of God, who is known by many names in many cultures.

This embodiment of Divine Compassion and Truth has come to your reality periodically throughout the ages to show the way back to God—the Holy of Holies. One name by which this Great Being of Light is known is Jesus. Another is Sweet Medicine, who walked among the Cheyenne. Yet another is White Buffalo Woman of the great People of the Red Earth, whom you know as Native Americans. The most recent experiences of the newly departed soul will determine his understanding of who this Divine Essence is. Many names, one being. Many paths, one destination — one destiny: to let go of anything that interferes with a total and complete surrender to God and His Love.

There is a universality found in other aspects of this Heaven World. As it contains the archetypal, perfected pattern from which your world arose, it is made up of jungles and deserts, forests and vast plains, streams and lakes and great sparkling oceans, grand mountains and gently rolling hills.

Each soul will enter this realm in the environment that feels the most comforting and welcoming and familiar — the most like home. There they will be greeted by those of their individual cultures and cosmologies. They will be welcomed and nurtured and instructed by these beings. And when they are ready, they will visit other environments and commune with other beings they find there. They merge their emotions and thoughts — their energies — one with another.

In this merging they weave a mystic tapestry of ever-changing colors, light, and sound, enriching the whole through freely shared experiences. Though each soul retains its individuality, its own unique texture and hue, it blends joyfully and smoothly with other souls to make a whole that is much greater than any single part could ever be. This tapestry of love is at the very Heart of God. Though God has many faces, He is One Essence, and that Essence is Love — pure, powerful, absolutely unconditional.

Differing languages are not an impediment to communication here. The "language" we use is the language of the heart, impervious to misinterpretation. There is complete and total understanding at all levels between souls.

Each soul radiates a light that is unique and individual — all its own, yet not separate from that One Great Light. Each soul is "dressed" in this light, which can take on any form that soul wishes. There is a great joy in the creation of beauty and a great playfulness—a great celebration—in the sharing of each other's experiences and wisdom.

Here we know the true ecstasy of consciously surrendering our individual wills to God's will. God's will is always that the good of the whole be served and enhanced and expanded. In this surrender, we do not lose our individuality. Rather, we are strengthened in our uniqueness by how that uniqueness fits into and enhances the whole.

We are many hearts all beating to the perfect rhythm of God's Great Heart in which is contained the whole of creation.

8

Ruth

At one of the sessions held with Helen, the spirit of a young woman who had committed suicide came to tell us her story. She was accompanied by an angelic presence. There was a certain sweetness and innocence about her. I opened myself and with great gladness conveyed her story to Helen. The gray day disappeared, and I found myself living the experiences of a young woman who took her last breath half a century ago.

My name is Ruth. At present I am awaiting incarnation into your reality. I last experienced life on Earth in the year 1942. At that time I was in deep despair over the loss of my husband, John. I loved him very deeply and with great intensity. He was my whole life. When his plane was shot down during the war and he fell into the sea, my world exploded into tiny pieces. I felt as if my heart had been ripped from my chest, the sky forever darkened.

I was twenty, living in Virginia. I was in my garden when they came to tell me John was gone. I did not believe them at first. Johnny was only twenty-two. We had just begun our lives together. I was carrying his child. How could I live without him?

The truth is, I did not want to live without him, and so two days later I drove a short way to the shore and I waded into the sea—the same sea that cradled his body far away across an endless expanse of cold grayness.

I wanted to be where he was so badly. I swam until I had no strength left. I was not a very good swimmer, and the waves were fairly rough, the waters icy cold. As the last strength drained from my numbed limbs and I was engulfed by another of the endless waves, I felt a subtle snap and found myself floating above my body yet still attached to it. I became terrified— "Oh, no! This isn't what I wanted . . . this is wrong, this is very, very wrong!" But somehow I could not make my body respond. . . . It was too late! Then I heard a loud ringing. It filled my whole being. The sound became deafening. I felt it pulling me away.

And then I saw the spirit of my child. I was five and a half months pregnant at the time. My child . . . floating like a beautiful light angel. I knew that this precious spirit would have been a girl. I had already picked her name: Suzannah, she would have been called, after my husband's mother.

I felt at that moment such an anguished grief for what would never be. I reached for my child, but just then two beautiful beings of light swept her up in their arms and carried her away.

An angel was there for me, too. Things around me began to grow dim. I could no longer see my body, although I could still feel the ocean and the earth. I was filled by a great fear. . . . "What had I done! Oh, God, what had I done?"

I was pummeled by despair and guilt and an overwhelming shame. I wanted so much, with everything in me, to make it not to have happened, to go back and do it differently . . . but I could not. My body was no longer viable, you see. My child was no longer there. Her spirit was gone. And the angel was now asking me to come with him but I was afraid.

I knew, I just *knew*, despite what he was saying, that this was not an angel of God, but a messenger from Hell, for how could I expect to go to Heaven? How could I be in the Presence of God after what I had done? So I did not trust this angel or his beauty.

Far ahead, in the dimness surrounding me, I saw an opening filled with the brightest light. It was through that opening that the angels were carrying my child. The angel at my side was telling me that if I would simply let go I, too, could pass through that same opening with him, but I did not believe him.

I knew I was bad. I knew I had done something unforgivable. I knew about Hell. My parents were religious and I had been taken to Sunday school regularly as a child. I remembered at this moment those lessons I had learned: that suicide is a mortal sin!

After a time — it could have been minutes or years spent suspended in this space between worlds, captured by my own guilt and fear, I began to long for my home and the garden I so loved. This was the Earthly place where I had experienced such happiness and joy with Johnny. Just as I thought these things, I was caught up in what felt like a great *whooshing* of wind. It then seemed as if I simply dissolved into this wind.

My next conscious awareness was of finding myself once more in my home in Virginia, looking out the window of the kitchen into the garden. The roses looked so beautiful to me. They were bursting with blooms, much more vibrant than I remembered them. The sun was shining through the window. I could see it, but I could not feel it. I was definitely there, but it seemed as if a thin film separated me from everything. I felt, in a way, as if I were dreaming.

There were people in the house I did not know. They were painting the interior walls, covering over the wallpaper with the blue flowers that John and I had put up just before he left. I wanted to stop them but couldn't seem to make them hear me. All the things I so loved — the pictures of John, my grandmother's chest, the blanket I was knitting for the baby — were nowhere to be found. The house was empty.

I then "thought" myself into the garden, for that is how it is — you think yourself from place to place. I accomplished this the first time purely by accident.

Previously, I had been moving through the house as I did before my death, using the doorways, walking around objects and people. However, soon I found that things were not solid at all to me and offered no resistance when I moved into or through them. This was very disorienting at first and very frightening.

I stayed in that garden for many years, watching the seasons change and people come and go. Yet, in many ways it truly seemed an endless time, like a dream from which I was powerless to awaken. I was filled with fear and remorse and regret for what I had done. I longed with everything in me for the arms of my husband and the little warm body of my child — the child who had never had a chance to feel the sun or see the roses or laugh or run, all because of me, because of what I had done. I was swallowed up in a void of deep, deep loneliness and excruciating pain.

All this time, the angel who had joined me in the ocean never left my side. Over the years I grew used to his presence and my fear of him lessened. I realized that he would not force me to do anything without my consent.

I watched a family move into my house. There was a little girl named Emily. She was so beautiful. . . . She could see me! We would play in the garden. She told her parents about me, but they thought that the "Ruthie" she spoke of so often was an imaginary friend.

I loved her, you see. I gave to her all the love and attention I wanted to give to my own daughter.

Years went by and after a time she could no longer see me, but I continued to follow her, to stay constantly by her side, even when she slept.

In this I did a great wrong. In my attachment to her, I not only shared with her the love I felt, I also unwittingly shared my sorrow. As a result, Emily carried a depression with her for many years, which she thought was her own. She also had an abiding terror of the sea, which she had absorbed from my experience. At the time I did not realize that it was I who was the source of her difficulties.

After years had passed, I began to listen more and more to the angel. I understood by now that he really *saw* me — he knew everything about me and still loved me deeply. Finally, I began to feel that love.

So one day I let go of the garden and my house and Emily, and I went with him. I surrendered myself into his care, even though I wasn't certain if we were truly going to where he told me we were. I still believed, you see, that I should be punished for what I had done — surely I would be punished! But I was ready to face whatever I had to. So I turned away from all that I had known and looked toward the great light.

Immediately, I was swept up in a ray of this light that reached out and cradled me and carried me. It was as if I were immersed in a river of spirits. My angel never left my side. He told me I would see everyone I ever loved in this light. I still did not believe him.

But when we reached the end of the tunnel, we did indeed enter Paradise, just as he had promised! It was beautiful beyond anything I could have imagined. I felt none of the condemnation I had expected — only acceptance and compassionate understanding.

And what great joy — John was there! He greeted me with a brilliant smile and an embrace, and in that one moment I understood many things.

John, along with my angel, took me to the most beautiful places I had ever seen. As we moved through these gardens and forests and shining meadows, I could feel the darkness and despair dropping from me like big, round weights being washed away in a river of light. The only thing I felt was love.

I asked about my child, Suzannah, and I was shown that she had been born into another family. This did not cause me sorrow however, but great joy — for her as well as for those with whom she had chosen to experience her life on Earth. I knew in that instant that we would never be truly separated. I could feel her in my heart, wound around my soul in ribbons of light.

Then I was taken to the door of a great and magnificent temple. The walls were of light. Inside stood twelve beautiful, *beautiful* beings. They were filled with love and total acceptance. There was no judgment. John could not come in with me and so waited outside. I had to do this alone.

I saw my life and through this I was healed. I learned that when I took my life it was not my time. I experienced the pain and confusion of those who had loved me on Earth — my parents, my friends — as the result of my actions. I saw all the possibilities for learning and growing and loving and helping others that I had thrown away through my decision not to continue my life. I felt the deep sorrow of the spirit of my child at the termination of our chance to be together on the Earth plane.

I then was shown that I would have an opportunity to go back to Earth and to relive similar experiences, only this time to make different choices, more appropriate choices. In this way, I would be able to complete the destiny path I had begun in the life just ended.

In that moment, I was finally able to forgive myself for what I had done. As I did this, I actually saw and felt my own light, the light that I was, becoming brighter in one intense burst of energy.

The life review is also where I learned of the effects of my actions on Emily. I immediately prayed that she be freed from any pain or suffering caused by my misguided attentions. I was assured that my prayers for her were being answered.

Today, I am still learning. There is so much to learn! John is always with me now. We have shared our separate experiences with each other and have grown from the sharing.

His experience of death was much different from mine, for he had no fear and went with gladness and all the excitement of the explorer that he is into this new territory.

Those of you who are still on Earth must realize that fear is the one thing that you have to transmute, above all other things. It is the force that empowers greed and lust and violence and hatred. It is the one thing that can create a contraction of the soul, which closes out love. I have learned this.

If I could wish anything for you, it would be that you, too, come to know this in your hearts, and that you go freely and with the trust and innocence of a child into God's arms when the time comes for you to leave your reality for this one. Thank you for listening to my story. I hope it helps you on your path.

I felt Ruth's soft presence leave my energy field. While she was there, I experienced what she was feeling; I relived her memories as she saw them. She had revealed to me her innermost essence, as would all of those souls who chose to participate in this project. I felt expanded by this deep knowing of another and very grateful for her willingness to open up so freely to us.

Her story brought up for Helen and me more questions about the concept of suicide. So after a short break we continued the session, asking the angels to enlighten us further on the subject.

As long as a soul is willing to learn and grow — to balance the imbalances that it may have caused as the result of inappropriate actions or decisions — that soul is never ultimately lost. This is the purpose of your reality: to learn responsibility for yourself and your actions. To learn how to be a responsible creator — always holding uppermost in your intent the good of the whole, how your action will affect all of creation.

What you call "suicide" — the deliberate termination of your own life — disrupts a pattern that was set forth and agreed upon by you as your chosen destiny. However, as always, one must examine not only the action itself, but the intent behind that action to determine whether it was appropriate or inappropriate.

If you deliberately give your life so that the whole may be strengthened in some way, or out of love for another, then it can be seen as an appropriate action, stemming from a clear, loving intent. If the action is taken out of fear, despair, denial, guilt, or any emotion arising from a contracted understanding, then it is inappropriate action.

All life is precious. Humanity is growing into an acceptance of this truth. All life is precious — not only human life, but the lives of animals and of plants and of all creatures that walk and crawl and fly and swim. The life of the Earth herself is most precious. You are all a part of that immense existence. There will come a time when you will not find it necessary to take a life — whether it be plant or animal or human — to sustain your own. However, at this time the belief construct uppermost in mass consciousness is that something must die so that something else may live.

Because of this belief, you have created, through the manipulation of genetics and breeding practices, animals that you term *domesticated* — cattle, chicken, pigs, sheep — whose sole purpose is to die so that humanity may ingest their bodies to sustain their own. These animals, with few exceptions, lead lives filled with pain and terror and suffering — far from the original soul pattern which God ordained for them.

This pattern was bent and twisted by man's will and the perceived need to control his universe. This need arose from a place of fear. Yet there is a great light coming to the hearts of humans that will offer an opportunity for the release of that fear. The souls of these humble, innocent creatures will then be freed to return to their original patterns of harmony in bodies that will also be in perfect alignment with that harmony.

There will come a time on Earth when your being will be sustained completely by light and love. However, until that time, you must take what life you need with reverence and an awareness of the sacred. This includes your own life as well. To destroy a holy vessel, a vehicle through which the essence of God can manifest on this Earth, for a reason such as fear, is a choice that is not conducive to the good of the whole or the individual.

However, this is not what you understand to be a sin. Sin in its original form simply meant out of balance. The soul is not rejected or condemned by God for such an action. When you take your life, any life, as the result of an inappropriate intent, you create an imbalance in your soul as well as in the whole of creation. That balance may be restored by choosing to face clearly the results of your actions, by learning right action from the experience, and then by incorporating this learning into your very soul and spirit so that it becomes an indestructible part of you.

If a soul comes into this life with a destiny that it has chosen for the good of the whole as well as itself, and then chooses to deny that destiny through the act of suicide, there will be an opportunity created to come back and fulfill that destiny — an opportunity to balance the imbalance created by inappropriate action. This does not mean, however, that you have to relive the experience literally. It does mean that you will have the opportunity to create, through right action, a healing of the imbalance that your previous actions created in yourself and on your planet.

It does not mean, for example, that one who has committed suicide must live through the same tragedy — the loss of a loved one to suicide. This is a gross misunderstanding of the workings of the universe and the generally held concept of *karma*: the idea that if you do something "wrong," you will have it done to you in the next life. This misconception is predicated upon a denial of God's great compassion and love. It is a negation of the free will of each individual to *lovingly* create balance, strength, and empowerment of themselves and the whole from imbalance. In this way, the cycle of pain and inappropriate action is broken. The patterns that are not conducive to the good of the whole or the individual are then changed forever. In the changing of these patterns in the self, the tendency for them to exist and have power in the whole is greatly lessened.

There are many ways to facilitate a healing of the suicidal impulse that exists in mass consciousness. For instance, one can become a counselor to those individuals who carry this tendency. One can help a friend to overcome fear and to make a choice that affirms life rather than one that destroys it. One can make the choice to face the difficulties and pain and challenges that sometimes occur on your planet with faith and love and a belief in the strength of the spirit to carry them through safely to the other side of an experience that previously led to the taking of their life.

So, you see, there are many forms through which this Divine balance may be created. This rebalancing of an imbalance is the essence of what you call healing.

9

David

Soon Helen and I were to encounter another soul who, like Ruth, became a "ghost" upon leaving his body. However, unlike Ruth, he had not yet found his way into Heaven but was still trapped in a confusing, nebulous world between worlds.

A very strange thing happened to me during this session. When we were through, Helen insisted that I listen to the tape. I usually do not do this because it sometimes disorients me, but she was persistent and so I agreed to let her play it back for me. As the session progressed, I heard my voice become that of a Southern youth, with the cadence and timbre of a boy in his early teens. I was astounded. I had been aware of a deeper merging of souls during this session, and, in fact, for days afterward I carried a great grief and love in my heart for this young man.

He was accompanied by Sandy and his angel. We were told that he died as a young man during the War Between the States. He fought on the side of the Confederacy and lost his life during the Battle of Franklin, in Tennessee.

My name is David. I am proud to serve under the great General Robert E. Lee. They tell us that this battle cannot be won. I do not believe that. We have to win. If we don't win, what will our families do?

What will Mama do? And Daddy already lost his life in Virginia. They wouldn't take me then. I tried to go with my daddy, but they didn't want me. Now, at the end, they've run out of boys, so they took me.

I'm proud to wear this uniform, even if it is a little tattered. I have to wear my own pants, and my buttons aren't brass, and I lost my hat somewhere back there. But, hey, they let me carry the flag!

My friend Josh is fightin', too, 'cept he's scared. I'm scared, too, but I don't let myself feel it. There's so much to do.

My head hurts. Awhile back, I was runnin' across the field . . . lots of smoke and shoutin'! That's when I felt somethin' hit me in the head, and I fell down. I don't know. . . . I really don't know what's happenin'. I was lyin' there on the ground, and Josh was . . . I could see him. He was shakin' me, tryin' to make me get up.

Next thing I knew I was standin' up, but somehow now I was standin' behind Josh. I was lookin' over his shoulder, watchin' him shakin' some soldier on the ground — and that soldier looked like me . . . kinda like me! But it can't — it couldn't be me, 'cause I'm here!

Anyways, I had to keep goin'. I couldn't stay there. It got kinda hard to see what was happenin' after that. I lost sight of Josh. I felt just like I did one time when I was really, really sick. Everything seemed like a bad dream; things looked like they do in dreams, too. But I was awake.

I could see other boys — some older men, too. It seemed like people were runnin' right *through* me! They were just runnin' *right through* me! They'd run at me and I'd think, "They're gonna hit me," and then they'd just run right through me like I wasn't even there. That's when I started gettin' real scared, 'cause I don't understand any of this.

There's this angel. I know it's an angel 'cause I seen pictures of 'em in my mama's Bible. He was tryin' to tell me I needed to leave and go with him. I'm afraid. I don't know what's gonna happen to Mama. I'm all she's got. I can't leave.

This angel-man, he took me over and showed me that body

Josh had been shakin'. It looked pretty bad for that soldier — his head all smashed in. He told me that boy was me, that was my body lyin' there so white and still!

I didn't believe him 'cause I'm here! I got hands, I got feet. . . . Heck, I've even got my uniform. *That body ain't mine!*

After a while, it got real quiet in that field. A lot of bodies, so many bodies lyin' around. That was when I noticed a lot of soldiers were leavin' with these angels. Not me! I was walkin' around, trying to find Josh. I didn't see him. He must have . . . I don't know what happened to him.

Things have changed an awful lot. The place I live sure is different now.

I went back to town after I couldn't find my buddy, Josh, in that field. It was nighttime when I got home. I saw Mr. Whitfield and I said "Hi!" He didn't say anything back, so I said it again — louder this time — but he still didn't say "hi," and he was lookin' right at me. That's when I knew nobody can see me. But I wouldn't let myself accept that.

When I got to the house, I tried to wake Mama up — she was sleepin' in the chair. She fell asleep in the chair, just like she always does — she works so hard now Daddy's gone. I couldn't wake her up. I yelled and hollered and jumped up and down, but she couldn't hear me . . . couldn't see me neither!

I didn't really know what to do then. I was cryin' pretty hard 'cause I was so scared and confused, and I didn't want Mama to know I was cryin', just in case she'd all of a sudden wake up and could see me. She hates it when I cry. She starts cryin', too, most times. That makes me feel real bad.

So I went back out to the field where we was fightin'. There was some soldiers still wanderin' around where the battle had been. And you know what? They could see me! They were just as puzzled about what was happenin' as I was.

Some of 'em were tryin' to fight each other, but their swords and guns had lost their killin' power. They still made a real racket but didn't do much else. Those soldiers looked kinda like they was sleepwalkin' — stumblin' all around!

Those angels, they were still there, too. Looked like there was one for each soldier.

I just can't accept any of this. I've been here — seems like a long, long time. Mama — well, she left. One day I went back home and she just wasn't there anymore. I don't know where she went, but I think she'll be back, probably any day now.

The world's really changed. There's all kinds of things happenin' I don't understand. It's like I'm dreamin', watchin' everything goin' on around me, but I'm not in the picture.

Sometimes I can get somebody to see me or hear me — just for a minute, sometimes. I've been to your house before, Lily, when you lived out on that land near the field where we fought. Me an' a couple of other fellas from that fight saw your light — it's like some folks got a real bright light around 'em. I learned that those are the ones that just might hear me.

Anyway, we made the door blow open, an' then I picked up the shell off your altar table and dropped it on the floor. That sure scared your boy! Remember that? I remember you. I know you saw me then, just for a little bit. You did, didn't you?

I don't know what to do. I keep tryin' to get people to see me. I just can't accept that . . . that I'm . . . that I'm dead. I'm only *thirteen*. I can't be dead!

Anyways, I came with this man here who brought me to you. He says his name's Sandy. He said you all would be able to hear me, and he was right! And now I know where you are, I'll come back — if it's okay with you.

Most of the guys where I am have gone on to the other side these angels keep tellin' us about. There were a lot of us here right after the big fight, but now there's not so many. Most of the time I'm really alone here, except for my angel.

I never did find Josh, and I sure do miss my dog. They say there's no dogs in Heaven. That's what my mama told me. She told me that when Rebel died. Just about broke my heart, thinkin' about my Rebel — bein' there one minute, the next bein' nothin' forever and ever. I didn't want to believe that, it just didn't seem right. Sandy says that what my mama told me isn't true. There *are* dogs in Heaven — cats and horses, too! He says I'll see Rebel again. I hope he remembers me.

Well, I'd better get back now, in case Mama comes home. Thanks for listenin' to me. I'm real glad you can hear me.

The angels then spoke to us about the plight of this young man.

David exists at this time at a level that is between worlds, between realities. Some in your culture refer to this space as purgatory, or limbo. It is a nebulous gray place of nothingness, separated from your reality by a thin veil. Put another way, it is a vibratory frequency that is neither at the level of your reality, nor is it included in the reality of the Heaven World. It is an unformed world peopled by lost and confused spirits and uncontrolled thought forms. It is a very real place, yet neither here nor there.

David, like many others, was caught there because he was not at all prepared for his transition. It was sudden and violent, abrupt and unexpected. He is very resistant to accepting the truth of his situation and has therefore entrapped himself in a space of confusion and chaos. This confusion dominates his world. He misinterprets many of his experiences there. Until he accepts the reality of his situation he cannot progress on to his next experience.

One cannot exist at the higher frequencies of the Heaven World and hold within one's being fear and the vibrations that accompany this contracted state. They must be healed through a careful process of patient nurturing and teaching until they are ready to willingly make the transition to a higher level.

We cannot force these things. It is against Universal Law. Such an action would violate that great gift of free will that God gives to each soul. All we can do is to be there, forever constant and without end, offering guidance and God's love. And that is what we will do for this young man until he is ready to let go of his attachment to your reality.

We have told him that his mother is already on the other side, waiting for him there. He refuses this truth also. He tells us that she couldn't be gone because he didn't get to say good-bye. He believes she is visiting friends or has moved away for a while and will return for him soon.

He is bewildered and frightened by the things he sees happening in your modern world. It is a never-ending nightmare from which he longs to awaken but does not know how.

Yet, we feel he is very close to coming with us into the arms of his mother, into the heart of God where all is made clear and whole and new. Pray for him. Your prayers will help to give him the strength to let go.

After listening to his story, I realized with a shock that I *had* "met" David before. It was just as he said. My son and daughter and I were living in a newly built subdivision on the outskirts of Franklin, Tennessee. I was aware of the presence of many spirits in that place.

On the night in question, although it was a calm, windless July evening, the back door flew open suddenly, and a bone-chilling cold entered the house. I could hear what sounded like a small army of boots clambering down the hall.

My son heard this also and ran into my room just in time to see the shell from my altar rise into the air as if it were being lifted by curious, invisible hands, examined carefully, and then very deliberately dropped to the floor. The clattering of feet then proceeded to go back down the hall and out the door, at which time the temperature of the house returned to normal.

Billy and I sat there, frozen in place. When I could tear my eyes away from that errant shell, I looked at his face. That poor little face was white as a sheet!

I rose to pick up the shell. Returning it as calmly as I could to its place on the table, I said, "It's okay, Billy. They aren't here to hurt us. They are boys who lost their lives in the Civil War. They're looking for attention, and I guess they got it!"

I knew the sad truth of this in my heart—I sensed their youth and confusion.

Billy, who has had similar encounters all of his life, was comforted by the fact that these "ghosts" were just kids and by the fact that despite all of his strange experiences with otherworldly beings, he has yet to be harmed.

We said a prayer for these boys, that they would soon find their way to their rightful place. I then went back to the book I was reading, Billy to his room. But it would be days before we no longer listened for that youthful clamor in the hall.

10
Joey

Hearing David's story made Helen and me wonder about other children. It is so hard to release a child to death. Is it as hard for them to embrace this experience as it is for us to accept their passing?

A spirit named Joseph came to help us better understand these things. He brought with him a sense of light and freedom, a sparkling purity, the essence of a child. And I was swept once again into a powerful experience of life and death and greater life. As he spoke through me, Helen recorded his story.

Hello! My name is Joseph. You can call me "Joey." That's what they called me the last time I "visited" your planet. I left in the winter of 1956.

I was six that winter. We lived in Minnesota. It had snowed. It was beautiful. I love the snow. It makes everything look all white and soft and sparkly.

I was with my father and Michael and Sally. Michael and Sally were my friends. They lived next door and they were older than me. My dad had taken us sledding. It was the first time I had been allowed to go. I had wanted to go before with my older brothers, but they wouldn't let me because my mother thought I was too little. My mom didn't want me to go this time, either, but my dad said I was old enough and that he would go with us.

My brothers, Donny and Billy, were much bigger than Michael and Sally and me. They were with the older guys at the top of the hill. My father had picked out a place for us to sled near the bottom of the hill and to the side that was better for us because we were smaller than the others.

It was so much fun! It was like flying — at least I thought that's what flying must feel like. The first time, I went down on the big sled with my dad in front, me in the middle, and Sally behind. Sally was screaming in my ear and then I started screaming, too! It was so much fun! I felt like there was a bird inside me. I felt really, really free.

It reminded me of something — I don't know what — something very special. I wanted to do it again and again. We went back up the hill. My dad let me help him pull the sled. Sally didn't help 'cause she's a girl.

When we got to our camp, Dad said it was Michael's turn. Sally said, "Can I ride with him?" And I said, "No, I'm gonna ride with him." So Sally let me go — probably because I think she liked me!

I got on the back behind Michael and held tight around his waist and we went down again. And it was the same thing — the greatest thing I'd ever done. It was just so . . . the greatest thing I'd *ever* done!

But the ride was over too soon. We went back up the hill again. My dad had gotten a fire going. He wanted to go to the car to get his thermos of coffee, so he said, "Now, don't you guys go anywhere. I'll be right back. And stay away from the fire." Then he walked back down the hill to the car.

I was watching the big guys farther up the hill. They had a longer way to go to the bottom, and I thought, *That must feel great!*

All of a sudden — I don't know what got into me — but I just started running up the hill. Sally yelled, "Joey! Don't do that!

Come back here!" I didn't pay any attention to her. I knew I shouldn't be doing it, and I knew I'd get in trouble but I didn't care!

I could see my brothers up there. I finally found them in the crowd. I ran up to Donny and I asked, "Can I ride with you?"

Don looked around and asked, 'Where's Dad?" and I said, "Oh, he's down there."

Donny asked, "Does he know you came up here?" That's when I lied and said, "Yeah, he knows. Can I ride with you, Donny? Come on, let me ride with you."

Donny said, "Okay, but you've got to hold on."

So I got on Donny's sled. It was smaller than the one I'd been riding on with Dad, and it went a lot faster. We started down the hill, going faster and faster, and then we hit this bump.

I thought I was holding on tight, but we hit this bump so hard. Then it was like I was flying up in the air, and the next thing I knew I was looking down at myself. There were people all around me and my head was bleeding bad, and Donny was crying and screaming, "Dad! Dad!"

My dad ran over and picked me up, and he said, "He's gone, Donny, he's gone. . . ."

My dad was crying. I'd never seen my dad cry before, and it scared me. I wanted to tell him I was *okay*! I didn't know how I was okay, but I *knew* that I was.

Just at that moment, I saw Gabe. Gabe's my friend. No one can see him but me. My mom used to say I had a great imagination when I would tell her about him, but he's real! Anyway, Gabe was there and he told me, he said, "Your dad's going to be fine, Joey. And Donny and Billy and your mom, they'll be fine, too. It's time to come with me."

I said, "Okay." I didn't know where we were going, but all of a sudden I wasn't worried anymore. I mean, I wasn't worried *at all*. And it's like that feeling of sadness that my dad was so sad and Donny was so sad—that feeling just kind of melted—it was gone!

Gabe's really beautiful. He looks like a grown-up little kid — that's what he looks like! He's an angel — I think that's what he is — though he's never said that. Anyway, I think he's an angel because he looks just like the other angels I've seen since I've been here.

He took my hand and turned me around and I saw this really bright light. Then we were moving very fast through this tunnel. It looked kind of black with lights flashing past us. And as I moved through the tunnel, I felt myself changing. It was like I was melting, but not melting in a bad way. Maybe like growing real fast and stretching like there was more of me there. That's what it felt like, kind of.

And then we were at the light. And then we moved through the light into the most beautiful place. I saw my grampa Dan — he's there. I was really, really happy.

Gabe and Grampa Dan took me to this big building that looks like it is made out of light somehow. We went in and there were all these really shiny people standing around. Grampa Dan said, "We're going to leave you now." But that was okay 'cause these people were wonderful people.

I started to feel really good. And then I got to see everything that happened to me when I was Joey. It was kind of like watching a great movie, except you're in it, too, at the same time. It didn't take very long. And when I saw it, I became more me. Things I didn't understand before I got here I understand now, and that understanding came when I looked back at my life with new eyes. It's like I could understand things better with these new eyes.

I also got to say good-bye to my mom then. It's like I thought of her and all of a sudden I wasn't in the room of shiny people anymore. I was in her room and she was sleeping, and I bent over and kissed her cheek and I whispered, "Good-bye, Mommy. I love you," in her ear.

You can say good-bye to people still on Earth right after you leave, you know. And if you forget someone, you have a second chance when you see your life in this special room.

It really wasn't that I forgot my mom — who could forget

their mom! It's just that I got so excited when I saw Gabe that all I could think about was wanting to go with him. They tell me that I'll see my mom and my dad and my brothers again, and I know that's true!

After I was through in this room, I said good-bye to the shining people. When I left that room I was different. My body wasn't little anymore and was glowing the same as everyone else's here. But I still felt like me inside. Just that there was more of me, sort of.

And then I saw this beautiful, beautiful man, and I just knew that it had to be Jesus. So I asked Gabe, "Is that Jesus?" And Gabe said, "Yes, that's Jesus, except we know him by many names here."

It's really hard to tell you how I felt with Him, but I'll try. It's just so big! It was a feeling I had felt before but had forgotten, and when I saw Him, I remembered. I remembered not with my head, but with all of me. It felt like He reached into my heart and turned my light up, and I was brighter. That's what happens when you're around Him — your light's turned up.

Here is not like there — here everyone is joined together, sort of . . . way deep down. There's no difference between you and Him or you and anybody. But it's not like you lose who you are. You finally know who you *really* are. And you can feel everything about a person, and that person can feel everything about you and about how you feel about them.

So when you are with Jesus, all you feel is perfect love. No matter what you've done or who you are, you are loved perfectly forever and ever. I wonder how we forget this when we come to Earth. It seems impossible to ever forget it now that I'm here. But I know that we do forget. And I know that there is a part of us that does remember, but in some people I think it's pushed way down. If you've ever had the feeling like you're homesick, only you don't know what it's for, this is what it's for. It's that memory inside of you that's homesick for this — this place, this love that never leaves you, love that's always there for you, forever and ever.

And that's my story. Thanks for listening to me.

*   *   *

The angelic beings then told us: "Remember not to be sad for the child who has to leave the planet early, because it is not that difficult for them. If you are sad, let it be a grief for yourselves and for the shadowland in which you live, where the Truth That Love Is All There Is has been forgotten."

11

Angelic Wisdom on Children and Death

$\mathcal{J}$oey's story revealed to us a child's view of the death experience. But why was it so much easier for him than for David or Ruth? Why was there virtually no resistance to this monumental change? Why was there no fear? And, probably most intriguing of all, what did Joey mean when he said that his body changed—it was no longer "little," but just the same as everyone else's in that heavenly realm?

Our angelic guides, as always, were patient and thorough in their explanation.

We would speak of children at this time, and the effect that this experience has upon them — how they make the transition which you call death.

Before the age of seven, the soul is not fully integrated into the physical body. The attachment to your reality is not complete and total, therefore the death experience is easy. Children have not forgotten their spirits' true home. Their awareness is not concentrated solely in their identity as an individual ego, separate from their surroundings, set apart from God. They have not forgotten their oneness with all creation or the innate fluidity of their being. Eternity for them is encompassed within each moment. All realities are valid and possible for them. For a time they retain an ability to see angels and to remember their past incarnations.

Around the age of seven, deep attachments begin to form to your world and most souls lose all conscious memory of the Heaven realm. This process of forgetting begins much earlier, however, sometimes within the first two years of life. The knowing that they are inextricably a part of that Great Universal Light gradually begins to fade. By the age of seven, with the exception of rare individuals, all awareness of their origins is erased, the truth of their immortality hidden deep within the recesses of their being, far from the reach of mass consciousness.

This process of forgetting is what makes it easier for souls to participate fully in their life process by becoming completely immersed in your reality construct. Just as the greatest actors in your world attain that greatness by developing an ability to set aside all awareness of life outside the theater for the duration of their time upon the stage so that they may totally and most convincingly become that character they are portraying, so it is with a life well lived to the fullest. For the greatest wisdom is attained not through observation, but through experience. In this way the soul ripens until it falls of its own accord from the tree of your world and into the hand of God. At that moment, all that was forgotten will be once more remembered.

However, it is not the process of forgetting the greater reality from which the soul came and to which it will return that is the primary source of difficulty during transition. Rather, it is the attachment to your reality that quickly follows this forgetting—attachment to people, places, and things, and to individual identity—that creates a resistance to the change which you call death, no matter the duration of time spent on the Earth plane. These attachments become a source of security and create a false sense of well-being. Any reality that does not include the object or idea to which the soul is attached then becomes a terrifying place, unknown and therefore fraught with danger, to be avoided at all costs.

The soul of a child, however, has not forgotten its oneness with all things. It knows it can never be truly separated from love. It can never be separated from that which is real. Therefore, the soul of a child moves freely and with joy and wonder through realities. It is not as attached to the physical plane. And, so, when something occurs to create an imbalance in the corporeal body that cannot be corrected, that soul moves very easily out of your world and the temple which has housed it, flies through the tunnel with a glad heart, and enters the Heaven World with total trust and without hesitation.

As a child leaves its body, its soul still reflects the size and shape and immature form of a child. However, a transformation begins upon entry into the tunnel that is completed after the life review. And with the completion of this transformation, the soul then possesses a body that you would call "adult," perfect and whole and made of light. Any imperfections or imbalances that may have been manifest in the physical temple housing the soul are washed away, made perfect and whole by this wondrous and powerful experience which you know as death. All that this greatest of healings requires is a willingness to surrender to God's Love, to let go of Earthly attachments to form or fear, and to walk with faith into the Light of the Divine in which all things are made new.

There is no age as you understand it in the Heavenly realm, no immature or imperfect forms. Instead, each soul reflects its true eternal, ageless presence — forever youthful and innocent, pure and perfect in its fullness and vitality. This body is made of light and is very fluid. It is not bound by the laws of space and time, which create such limitations in your reality.

Children do not forget this easily. They have not fully lost their identification with this eternal aspect of their being. They are naturally unafraid of the unknown. Whatever fear they do experience, they pick up by merging with the adults who are designated their caregivers on Earth. Instinctively, they know the safety that awaits them on the other side. If they do have a fear of death and the afterlife, it is a learned fear and one that is easily shed once the process of death begins. Accepting the process is simple for them because such learned concepts have not had very many years to create strong and powerful patterns of contraction and resistance within the body and soul.

Children go joyously into the Light because they have not forgotten who they really are — ageless, eternal beings of limitless innocence and wisdom and love.

12

Jonathan

*A*t one memorable session, two magnificent angels appeared to Helen and me. Standing between them was one of the most beautiful young men I have ever seen. It was as if he were filled with sunshine: glowing energy radiated out from him in all directions. This golden youth, we were told, was awaiting his next incarnation, which was imminent. I recognized his energy as that of one of spirit twins soon to be born to two very dear friends of mine. They had been drawn together by an overwhelmingly powerful force, which they could neither deny nor resist. They are both unique and independent individuals, and their relationship up until now had been rocky, at best. Yet, despite their difficulties, they wanted these children desperately. Jonathan's story is one of the mystery of birth and of the indestructible connections of the spirit that extended far beyond a single lifetime.

My name is Jonathan.* I whispered my name in my mother's ear and she has heard me. I am coming to your world at this time to fulfill a most sacred mission — a task I have

---

*The names are changed to protect the privacy of these brothers born recently on Earth.

agreed to with great gladness. I am incarnating with a partner, who is to be my brother.

His name is Patrick. He did not come with me today, but chose to stay close to our mother, for her time is near. This is not the first life we have experienced together in your reality.

"We love our mother and our father very much. Together, my brother and I will teach them many things that their souls wish to learn. They have long prayed for us to come to them, but we have had to wait until their separate paths became one path before we could answer their prayer. My brother and I have direct and deep soul connections with our parents that span many lifetimes. We are all a part of the same soul group. We share similar paths, similar life lessons — our individual experiences complement and enhance the soul development of the other members of our spirit family. We have been many things to each other. We have all played many roles to help the others learn and grow in awareness.

What does it mean that my parents, my brother, and I are of the same soul group? Group souls are groups of beings who have chosen a similar destiny, and they have agreed to help each other manifest that destiny for the greater good of the whole. They may incarnate together many, many times. However, due to certain circumstances, all souls in a group do not always choose to incarnate at the same time. In these instances, those who choose not to take a body serve as guides in spirit for those who are experiencing physical existence. For we are eternally united.

So it is that I have never been truly separated from the souls who are to be my mother and my father in this lifetime. I have been with them from the beginning of time.

I have chosen to come to your planet to help with the transitional leap in evolution. I have gathered much wisdom, many spirit tools over many lifetimes to bring to this incarnation. With these tools and this wisdom I will build a destiny through which I may serve the whole of creation. I have been a healer in many of my experiences as an individual soul. Between incarnations, my learning continued in the Heaven World. I spent much time there communing with souls who have also followed the path of the healer — one of perfecting and balancing the physical body so that it may become a blessed vehicle and shining temple for the spirit. Part of the wisdom I will carry into this lifetime concerns the sacred healing power contained within certain herbs and plants — how to utilize this power through new forms, thus creating alternative ways to restore harmony and balance to a body that has become chaotic or weak, diseased or in pain.

Another aspect of my mission concerns teaching humanity to live in harmony with the spirit of the land and with the other creatures who inhabit her. I am to help heal what has been broken on your planet. Both my mother and father, through their many Earth walks, have accumulated much wisdom, which will aid them in living outside of society, self-sufficient and at one with Nature. My brother and I will bring more wisdom to add to this awareness. Together we will help many people return to the love of the Earth, opening their minds and hearts to the truth and fragile beauty, the great and priceless worth of the planet you call home. We will teach people to listen to what the winds and waters, the trees and the animals whisper and sing, and to honor their message. We will help them to find the wisdom contained within the depths of their bodies, and then to utilize that wisdom to live a life filled with limitless strength and light in joyful service to the whole.

As you can see, I do not appear to you as an infant. My soul's body is made of light, perfect and whole and ageless, as is yours. Yet, when I am born into your world, my spirit will fill the immature form of a newborn child, helpless and soft and dependent on those around him for sustenance. Even now I am molding that physical temple so that I can best serve God. I am developing certain traits and abilities in the physical form, which will help me to achieve my Destiny. This is a major task for every soul prior to incarnation. Each spirit is drawn to its mother at the point of conception — sometimes even before conception occurs. That spirit then guides the development of the fetus so that, indeed, the spirit is not an outgrowth of the body, nor is it ever separate. Rather, the body is an outgrowth, a projection of the soul, a reflection of what the soul requires of a physical body in order to learn its particular lessons, to fulfill its unique destiny.

When we are born we know everything, and then we must forget most of what we know until it is time to remember. This forgetting is gradual. We never lose the deep soul memory of who we really are and what we came to do and where we have been. We do all that we can while in Heaven to ensure that we do not totally forget these things once we have entered your reality. We spend much time in preparation for this great opportunity to serve on Earth. Merging with the Truth, we are immersed in the Love of God so that we carry this awareness with us into our next life. It is this Truth, this Love, which fuels the very life force, that ensures the remembrance of our divine purpose and origin.

I am most eager to begin my work. But I am aware that it will not be easy. There is much resistance to the Truth in your world, and because of their time spent in your reality, this resistance has found a home in the hearts of my mother and father as well. They have forgotten the Truth, but my brother and I will give them many opportunities to remember. They are filled with sadness and confusion. They have been battered by life, pulled into mass consciousness and away from God Consciousness, blinded to the Truth that Love is all there is. When they do remember — and I know they will — together we will help many people. Together we will heal each other, for we have done this before. And each time we do we become filled with a greater light, which lifts us up ever closer to what God would have us be.

It is very beautiful where I am, beautiful beyond all imaginings. But I also see and honor the great beauty of the world in which you live. I know that life can be filled with pain and confusion, sorrow and despair, where you are, for I remember this. However, those difficulties are seen from this perspective as great and precious jewels, for they create a quickening in the evolution of the soul, and this holds a universal value beyond all measure. You have been given a great opportunity in the divine gift of a life spent learning in your reality. Do not take it lightly. Learn from your experiences.

Be open to everything. Do not be afraid to feel and to grow from these feelings. It is this openness that will eventually bring to you the greatest treasure of all—the wisdom that you are a part of God, never separate from ecstatic, transformational, undying, everlasting Love. There is nothing within you that is real that is not Love; there is nothing without you that is not Love.

13

Angelic Commentary on the Reincarnation of Souls

*A*s Jonathan ended his message, I watched him follow a ribbon of light back to where I knew his mother and the spirit of his brother were waiting. One of the angels who had accompanied him remained, however. This wise and gentle presence had more to share with us.

The spirit of a child, although it is ageless and ancient and very wise, is also innocent. It has come to its incarnation through a process of cleansing and rebalancing and harmonizing. It has released the dross it may have accumulated as a result of its experiences in previous incarnations, so that only the wisdom and skills gained from those experiences remain.

The soul then transfers this wisdom, these perfected abilities and skills, into the cellular memory of the physical body that it chooses to inhabit. It carefully selects its parents according to soul affinity, as well as genetic potentials, so that it will have every available opportunity to complete its destiny.

The spirit is always pure and innocent and clear. However, there may be times when the soul experiences of a previous life are not fully resolved. That soul may then need more time to work on a particular issue so that it may transmute accumulated, unresolved emotions into wisdom through a learning process. In these instances, those emotions, wounds, and darkness that remain in the soul's memory are carried into the next incarnation in order to balance the imbalances from which these emotions arise. Sometimes this is the only way in which the soul can fully heal.

So, as unresolved attachments and emotions of the previous incarnation begin to surface in the soul's consciousness, the very cells of the still developing physical body will mirror those memories. These patterns are programmed into the subconscious and can sometimes manifest as physical or emotional imbalances and difficulties to serve as a reminder of the work that the soul has to do. Some of these imbalances may take form in the body while it is still developing in the womb. Others may not appear until later in life, when circumstances may trigger deep memories of similar experiences in other lifetimes, which led to the contraction or imbalance that needs to be addressed.

In facing these challenges successfully, the soul creates balance and harmony within itself and in the whole as well. This creation of harmony and balance out of imbalance is a part of the destiny of that soul. However, the task of creating a healing for itself from difficult circumstances — to accept its destiny and interact as a warrior from a place of strength and great courage rather than to shrink from these difficulties by choosing the path of a victim — is a choice each individual must make. You are in possession of one of God's greatest universal gifts — that of free will. You can use this free will to choose how you react to your experiences while on Earth. Each choice you make will then be reflected in the increase or decrease of Light in the soul.

As Light is increased in even one soul, so it increases the Light of the Universe. Reincarnation is about increasing this Light, this Love. Every time one learns and grows from their experiences into a place of more wisdom and unconditional Love, then the vibrational frequency of the Whole is raised. More Light is emitted, more Love felt throughout the Cosmos. Each time one person makes the choice in a situation to act out of Love, they move closer to God. In this way, the whole of mankind moves closer to God. Each life lived for the purpose of learning from the past, transforming that learning into wisdom, and then bringing that wisdom back into your reality to be refined and added to and enhanced through further experience, benefits the Whole.

Reincarnation is a choice. It is but one option of many that each spirit is given as to how it may evolve. There are many options, many paths. Reentering your reality to experience life there more than once is but one of these paths. Your reality is very dear to us and unique in many aspects. It is this uniqueness that has created within many souls a special affinity and affection for your world as a place in which to learn and grow. These souls choose to incarnate again and again in order to increase their spiritual Wisdom. Even after a soul has learned all that it can from your reality, it may choose to return as a great teacher, to continue its evolution for a time in that way. There are souls who experience life in your world but once and then choose to further their growth in other realms and other ways. However, in the end, all experience leads back to the Divine Womb — to God, who is Infinite and who loves all things and who blesses all paths.

14
Michael

*O*ne hot Santa Fe night, I was awakened by the presence of a young man standing by my bed. In my half-asleep state, I thought for a moment he was actually a living breathing person. This was obviously disconcerting and more than a little frightening, until I realized he was one of my friends from the other side. (I have always been much more wary of those who are still living. They have a greater capacity to frighten me than any disembodied spirit I have ever met!)

Although he had left his physical body and was now in a much finer, less dense form, he seemed so real that I felt I could actually reach out and hug him if I so desired. He flashed his great smile and said, "They told me you needed help with this book of yours. Well, here I am!"

I immediately fell in love with this guy. His story is intertwined with that of the young woman, Li, who presented herself to me a few days later. Together, their life experiences form a powerful testament to the resilience of the spirit and its ability to create something of greatness and beauty from even the most horrendous tragedy.

My name is Michael. I was ready to die when my time came. I'd been a walking dead man for a long, long time, so when they came for me, I didn't fight it. I just let go. Didn't know what was going to happen to me. Didn't care, either. At that point, I was just really tired. Tired of the nightmares. Tired of the pain. Tired of trying to push back an ocean of misery.

My life wasn't always hell. And, in fact, even after the war, there were some good days. But I'm getting ahead of myself. I guess you need my story from the beginning. That way, you can maybe make some kind of sense out of something that seemed so senseless at the time.

The senselessness of that war! So many mangled. So many dead. Destroyed bodies. Destroyed minds. And for what? I still don't know what the whole thing was about.

I know what they told us . . . all of us. I knew I loved my country. I knew I wanted to do what was right. But a part of me didn't feel good about the war. And after I arrived in that foreign land, I found out something was very wrong with the whole idea of us being there in the first place. There was no sense of purpose, really . . . just to kill and destroy the enemy. But most of them turned out to be small brown people — men, women, even little kids — who seemed more scared and confused than we were.

I was just a kid myself . . . eighteen in 1968 . . . and, like most of my buddies over there, all I'd thought about before this was how to make my Mustang go faster, and how to get the girls to want to take a ride in it with me. I'd never even seen a dead person before, except at my granddad's funeral. I lived in the Garden of Eden — American style. In my head I knew I'd marry Susan and have a kid I could teach to play ball, and maybe one day take over my dad's chili farm: he grew the hottest, best chilis in all the Southwest.

And then came the draft, and the lottery, and my number came up. Next thing I knew, I was in an honest-to-God jungle with sweat rolling off me so fast I couldn't see, crawling on my belly, scared out of my mind. I just wanted my mom.

I'd never killed anything in my life before this. I remember when I was twelve, my dad took me hunting. He got a deer. I cried for two days in my room after that, when I was sure no one could hear me. To see something so beautiful and free and kind of magical die like that . . . I told myself then that I would *never* deliberately take the life of man or animal. Not me.

Yet, there I was in this hellhole, blowing away people I didn't even know, left and right. They turned us into killing machines. Most of us, including me, took to drinking heavily and doing drugs to try to handle it. It was pure horror, the kind you will never experience in any movie, 'cause it's up there on the screen, and you're safe in your soft seat in the darkness with your girl or your kid beside you eating popcorn, and you know you can just get up and walk out any time you want to. But we *were* the movie, and the only way we could leave is if we were discharged or disabled or dead . . . the three D's.

It was like the whole world was blowing up over and over again. And every time it did, my insides would blow up with it. Until one day, it all just stopped. Everything kept going faster and faster, more and more out of control, a blur of heat and bugs and screams and blood, until the day I stood looking down at that little girl. She couldn't have been more than eight or nine.

We had been ordered to burn a village and destroy everything because they had been "harboring the enemy," and we all knew—even if it wasn't said—that meant we were to kill anyone we found, no matter what age or sex. At that point, I don't know what I was anymore . . . a monster, maybe. Whatever I was, it wasn't human.

Anyway, there was this girl, and she was running away. She ran past me, and I turned my rifle on her. I got her in the leg. I was never a great shot. Just fired into the air and hoped I got something before it got me. She fell and lay curled up on her back, so little and thin. She was bleeding to death and she was silent, looking up at me with these big brown eyes. Fear had pushed the innocence and hope that should have been there right out of her. The Earth stopped turning in that moment, and I just stood there, watching her die, staring up at me as if I were her worst nightmare. Then, it all changed, and she looked through me like she was seeing something else . . . something holy . . . and she smiled at that something, and she was gone.

There in the middle of that jungle, I remembered the deer. Her eyes reminded me of that deer when I was a kid. All the strength drained out of me, and I was on my knees beside that little girl. A red pain, a white hot flame was burning up my soul. I heard someone screaming. For a minute, I couldn't figure out who it was. . . . It was me, screaming out all the terror and rage and helplessness and senselessness of it all. Anguish for that girl, who would never laugh again or get to grow up. Anguish for the boy who cried for the death of a deer. Grief for that boy, who was dead now; for everything that was dead and would never ever come back.

After that, the really bad dreams started. I was drinking everything I could get my hands on, but it didn't work anymore. I don't know how much longer I could have made it over there, but—lucky me—soon after looking my personal Armageddon in the face, I caught some shrapnel in my gut and I was discharged.

After I got home, I found I was still in Hell. It looked different, but it was Hell, all right. The nightmares never stopped, and I was being eaten alive by the guilt dragon. I never slept, and for a long time I stayed in my room with a bottle and my personal demons. After a while, I moved out because I refused to torture my parents any longer with something they couldn't begin to understand.

My dreams were dust. How could I even *think* of marrying some sweet girl and having a family? I was a baby-killer, a destroyer of the innocent. Just the sight of a kid anywhere and it would start up again—a torture much worse than anything I ever thought I would have to feel.

And where was God, anyway? Why was I alive and that little girl dead? I was a certified crazy for a good number of years.

Then one day a therapist I was seeing, to make my mom

happy, asked me a question. She said, "What would it take for you to forgive yourself? That girl is gone. Your suffering won't bring her back. But there are so many other children — motherless, homeless, hungry, in pain — who need help desperately. And they aren't going to get it unless someone is willing to see their needs and address them."

Whoa! Right there, a little light went on in my head. It was real dim at first. But as the days went by, it got brighter and brighter. Until, one day I just woke up and started my very own crusade, vowing to fight the world's insanity until I could fight no more.

My demons never did leave me, but they got real quiet sometimes. Like when I was dishing out food to mamas and their babies at the church soup kitchen, or playing daddy to kids who never knew theirs — seeing their eyes light up when that bat connected with the ball for the very first time. Or when I made the kids laugh by singing silly songs to them on my volunteer days in the children's ward at the hospital.

Then, I would go home at night and cry until I fell asleep. My eyes had been opened to the magnitude of the suffering of those kids, and there was no way I could ever close them again. No matter how hard I worked, or how long, there was still so much left undone. I stopped drinking — there was no more time for that — even though at this point, my soul was terminally raw.

The night I died, I was driving home from a meeting with some friends who were trying to raise money to help rehabilitate high school kids who'd gotten into trouble with drugs. I was thinking about me at that age, when everything was still all shiny and new, and every good thing possible. Then I slammed into a solid wall made of the sound of breaking glass and the screech of twisting steel. The next thing I knew, I was soaring right out of that windshield like a guided missile headed straight for the pavement. Funny though, I never felt a thing. I guess I was in shock, and before it could wear off, before I even hit the ground, something like a huge hand just reached inside and snatched me right out of my body. The world disappeared, and I was standing in this field of bright light with a couple of very impressive angels!

I remember I was overwhelmingly glad to see them, and I said something like, "What took you guys so long?" They asked me if I was ready to go with them. I said I'd been ready for a long time. I didn't know what they were going to do with me, but I was willing to face the music, no matter what tune was playing.

We started to move through the light. A sound, very high-pitched, seemed to be propelling us faster and faster until I felt the outline of who I was blurring. And then, I was filled with an ecstasy I thought I would never experience . . . ever. Not after what I'd done. Yet there it was. I knew what it was, too. No one had to tell me. . . . It was God's Love.

It's really unbelievable how much we can go through and still not lose this. We can't lose it because — in spite of what it looks like when we are in the middle of our lives and over-whelmed by the sheer confusion of what our choices have created — love is what we are. It's what we are made of.

It was this revelation that helped me to survive what came next. I relived every excruciating second of my life. I felt every single bullet that left my gun as it tore into soft, unprotected flesh, ripping apart the insides of each one of those countless, faceless targets. Only now they had a face, and that face was mine. Their pain and terror . . . it was all mine now. I saw my-self through the eyes of that helpless girl that day in the jungle. What I saw was beyond horrendous.

I was expecting this part — this punishment. I thought it would go on and on throughout time . . . an endless atonement for unforgivable sins. What I didn't expect was what came next. For that torture did eventually end. I then became all the people I had helped — all the mothers and children I had made a little safer, all the kids I had given confidence to in a world that seemed to take pleasure in stealing that confidence from them. When I saw myself through their eyes, what looked back at me was not a monster, but a wounded man with a good heart and a lot of love.

I couldn't believe it was me. But it was. I could only pray I had made a difference. When I was alive, I refused to even consider this possibility. It might have looked too much like forgiveness, and I wouldn't let myself go anywhere near that luxury. Now I was coming closer to letting up on the self-torture. Close, but not there yet.

My life review had painted a portrait of a sort of dark and powerful beauty. It showed me the importance of listening to those deep, gut feelings, and then having the courage to follow them, no matter what happens. Even if it requires a sacrifice of the things that mean the most to you. Even if it creates discomfort and ridicule. If I had only had the courage and awareness to listen when that inner voice had told me not to show up for my induction into the Marines. But from the point of view I now had, I saw the innocence of the young kid that I was then. I saw his passion to believe in the goodness of his country and the rightness of all things. I saw his desire to be brave, to be a man, to do his duty to God and his country.

Now I know things are never that simple. . . . They are never black and white. God's laws are not always the same as the laws of man. It is the true responsibility of each of us to keep our head clear and our heart tuned to station G.O.D. Because that's the only place where we will get the true story — the one that tells us how we can really best serve God and our country — and the world, too, while we're at it. We are all related by the blood of our shared humanity. Behind all the governments and the politics, there are a million little girls with big scared eyes, who need protection and love in a world that will only be safe from monsters in men's clothing when we learn to listen to God. He's waiting to lead us all to common ground.

I don't know how long it took for me to finish this part of my introduction to eternity. It felt like the exam at the end of life school. But I wasn't worried if I had passed. I knew I wasn't being judged. It was more like a test that shows you that you aren't so dumb after all! As long as you are willing to learn from your mistakes, you can't make any. Funny, isn't it, how we think God is so judgmental, when we are the ones who are the judges? God understands and forgives. And keeps on loving, no matter what.

After a while, I found myself in this outrageous garden. The two big guys who brought me through the light were my constant pals, and I was really glad they were still with me. I wish I could make you understand what it was like to be in such peace after so much pain and turmoil, and how it felt to experience this incredible love, when you thought you would never again be deserving of it. I was so open and vulnerable — and all right with that. It didn't feel dangerous or foolish at all. I could trust again. I was even beginning to trust myself!

There were all these beautiful, happy people who passed us as we walked in this garden. Every time they came near, an enormous wave of Love and acceptance would wash me clean. I felt really connected for the first time. I was a part of all these wonderful people. They loved me!

Then, I saw an incredibly beautiful, graceful young woman with shining blue-black hair, of slender build. She moved toward me like a dancer, joy surrounding her like a rainbow. She looked at me with the huge, deep, dark eyes of a fawn, and I knew who she was — my torturer and my dearest teacher — my little jungle girl.

"When you offered help to those who could not help themselves, you were helping me," she said. "When you comforted those who were suffering and afraid, I was comforted. When you poured your love out to those who needed it the most, you were loving me."

Her words were like a rare and priceless balm poured onto the near-fatal wounds of my spirit. Then, she held out to me one single, perfect, pure white rose.

"Please take it," she told me, "and with it my forgiveness." She smiled at me, a smile of such radiance, and then in a blinding flash that lit up the whole universe, she was gone.

Right there, my head and my heart exploded into a thousand shards of Love, and in my soul a bird began to sing. That bird hasn't stopped singing yet. My beautiful girl — the spirit of the starved child I thought I had destroyed — showed me that, although actions which create great harm should never be forgotten, they can be learned from. In learning these lessons, in accepting the responsibility of making things as right as we can, something healing and good can come of something really bad. Nothing of true goodness can ever be destroyed, can ever die.

Yeah, in my heart, that old bird is still singing . . . and the song is really something!

*L*i came to me soon after Michael, during an early evening meditation. My dog sensed her first, running over to stare intently at the
empty air in front of me. The room was infused with the energy of
an enlightened soul. She took me on a great journey, while my dog
stood by my deeply relaxed body. When I returned, I recorded her
story.

Li's experience was probably one of the most difficult to translate.
Finding the words to convey what she showed to me, describing the
realm from which she came, was very nearly impossible. She seems
to have gone farther in her afterlife journey than the other souls who
shared their stories. Certainly her cultural background was less familiar to me. Yet where she took me felt just as wonderous and filled
with hope and transformative, freeing Love.

I come to you out of the heart of the One. I am in the gentle
wind that caresses your hair, and in the howling monsoon. I
live beneath the clear, calm surface of a still pond and in the
tumbling waters of a laughing brook. I am the tired leaf that
falls to the ground, and the iridescent wing that lifts the but-
terfly. I am in the brilliance of the smiling sun, and in the
blessing of the great pearl moon. You can hear me in the song

of the nightbird and the cry of a child. I am nothing, and I am everything.

But once I believed I was a girl, and so that is what I became, forgetting everything else. I grew very small, my spirit distilled into a single point within the soul of a child in a deep, green jungle, who knew nothing of the vastness of who she really was. I will tell you the story of that girl, and what she learned, and how she found her way home.

As a child, I was always running, running for the joy of it, for the freedom. I thought if I could only run fast enough, my feet would one day leave the ground, and I would fly up among the green-gold leaves with the brightly colored birds. I felt much more like a bird than a girl.

I was born late to my mother, who died when I was barely two, so my auntie became my mama. She was good to me, and I loved her desperately, but my ways caused her many nights of sleepless worry. I was forever wandering away from our village, always looking for new excitement, for the magic held in the twisted shape of an ancient tree, in the whisper of the dancing leaves. . . . What were they saying? I was always listening for the voice at the heart of each stone, for the high, sweet song of the Earth. I was always looking for that door that would open up and invite me into the mystery and beauty that I knew lay like a shining, jeweled kingdom just beneath what I could see with my eyes.

I was a thin child. It was as if I many times forgot I lived inside this small body. And when I did remember and chose to eat, it was only fruits and roots and rice and green things that I would accept. I refused to eat any animal. In my village, people raised pigs and chickens and goats and dogs. They were food to them, but beloved friends to me. How could I eat my friends? Many times I would try to save them, sneaking them away deep into the jungle. But they would, most of them, only find their way back, trusting blindly that home was their safe place, when the only thing they ever found there was eventual treachery and early death.

I was born into a land of war. The soldiers had been there

for a long time, my auntie said. But, as we lived in an isolated village, for a while we were safe; or so I believed. Sometimes, I saw the large silver metal birds and the things that looked like giant locusts in the distant sky, a constant reminder of a strange world that I would never understand. My auntie called them killing machines, and every evening she would light a candle at our village shrine to ensure that they would never find us.

Every few months, soldiers from the north country would pass through and take over our village for a few days, eating our food and often abusing our old ones and the young women. They looked like us, but their eyes were hardened and cruel. When they were here my auntie would hide me in the root cellar, where it was cool and dark. There I would pass my days, dreaming dreams until it was safe to come out again. In these dreams, I would be flying through bright lands filled with scarlet flowers and laughing people, until I came to a vast night sky, where every star had a name, where each star knew mine. These dreams felt more real than my own life, which was becoming frightening and confusing as the war moved closer.

When I asked what made the men so cruel, and why the war was happening, my auntie would tell me that war was never an easy thing to understand. She told me of a time when she went to the city to live for a while, and of the soldiers she met there. These were not the same as the soldiers I had seen in our village. They were from a place called France, far, far away. They were like giants, she said. Many of them had skin as white as the clouds. Her son, my cousin, who was now a grown man, had gotten his sky-eyes, my auntie told me, from her time with one of these soldiers. He had been kind to her; given her pretty clothes and chocolate that was, she said, like eating Heaven.

But he had left long ago, and now there were more giants with bigger killing machines, swarming through the jungles and the cities like a million ants. They were from a place called U.S.A., even farther away than the place called France; and even though they told the people they were here to protect us, my auntie was not so sure of this. She had heard too many stories, she said. "And," she said, "if you ever see a soldier who looks like a white giant, start running and don't stop, no matter what. I've heard such stories!" And she would lower her head, her hands covering her eyes as if she were trying to bolt out the unimaginable scenes these stories had created in her mind.

But I was still young, and every day held for me an eternity, and so I easily forgot the horror that was surrounding our village, slowly closing off the fresh air of freedom and hope like the inescapable coils of a silent, deadly snake.

That final morning I woke with the sun in my eyes. My dreams were almost always good, but this night I was visited by one of the really bad ones. I had had this dream many times, and each time it was exactly the same. . . . I would be running, running away from something so awful that I was afraid to look. But this awful thing was everywhere and there was no place of safety.

Then in front of me would rise up a huge man with a horrible, long gun. At first, I thought he was my friend, come to save me from the awful thing, but when I looked at his face, I realized he *was* that thing. There was no place to hide, and I knew that I was going to die. Every time this dream visited me, I would feel strange and disconnected from my world for hours.

The fog of that dream was still upon me when I heard the first jarring pops of a rifle, ripping apart forever the fabric of my life. Then, in the few seconds of silence before this sound was echoed by the screams of a hundred small viscious, silver missles hungry for blood, I thought frantically, "I can't hear any birds!" After that there was no more time to think, and the only thing to feel was terror.

Everyone was running and falling and dying. I was running, too . . . running and running. I saw a small puppy I had adopted as my latest little friend and confidant. Just yesterday I had sat in the dirt by the door of my auntie, holding his soft round body close to my heart. He was my baby, and I had wrapped him in an old rag, which in my mind became a beautiful woven blanket of many colors. I kissed his little head and he had looked up at me and gently licked my nose. I had giggled at how silly he looked. Now, I watched in horror as this sweet puppy turned into a flying crimson spray of fur and flesh. I looked for my auntie, but I could not see her anywhere.

It was as if my body had a mind of its own. Bent on survival, it continued to run, until a soldier lifted his gun and pointed it at me, and I fell. My leg had stopped working, but I could feel nothing at first. And then the pain came like a great crimson wave, and I could not move.

I looked up at the soldier, who was just standing there, staring at me, and I knew him. He was the man in my dreams. I realized then that this terror had come for me at last. The horror and fear I felt at that moment overwhelmed even the great pain pounding through my body. I could not look away from his eyes. Everything else began to fade. I lost all feeling in my body, all awareness of the earth beneath me. The only thing that remained was the sight of this man's eyes, staring into mine.

Then, something changed. One moment, I was a girl frozen in fear by the eyes of a monster who was her destroyer; the next moment I saw that the monster wore a mask, as did the girl. Behind those masks were two spirits who were really one heart. And that heart was overflowing with so much love, it swept me up and out of the pain and fear, and then I was flying—a bird of pure spirit—above my green jungle and into a great light.

My dreams as that girl had been an echo of my soul's remembrance of this, the ultimate freedom. As I traveled through this realm, I realized that I was not alone. My journey was being shared by a great spirit being. This being felt like a part of me, and although there appeared to be a separateness, there was in fact a true oneness of mind and heart and soul.

Moments ago, I had seen with the eyes of a young girl and understood what I saw through the mind and emotions of that girl. Now my awareness had expanded rapidly, and with expansion came the memory that I had made this journey many times before, and always with my present companion, my beloved spirit guide and teacher.

We were moving rapidly through this living light. I was being swept farther and farther away from all that I had believed I was, toward who I had always truly been. I felt as if I were one of the colorful little birds I used to watch flying through the emerald canopy of the jungle, a thing of wild and exotic beauty that had been too long caged. The door to that cage was now opened forever, and I was freed from the confines of my body.

The only thing that now had the potential to limit me was my mind, and the beliefs and fears that I had adopted as truth. These beliefs, desires, and fears, all children of my consciousness, I knew could present themselves as entities of very real and powerful substance. I now had to face them, and take back the power I had given them, so that nothing of me remained caught in that Earthly prison by attachment.

We had moved to a place far beyond the limitations of time and space, and so this facing down of my creations — both good and bad — seemed never-ending. I encountered here many forms: some terrifying, appearing to possess a deadly force capable of great destruction; others were alluring forms of great beauty and seduction. The power they hold, though confined to this level, is very real. They were created and continue to exist due to the strength of my beliefs, as well as that of countless other souls.

I saw many who are trapped here, halted in their holy progress, immobilized by their fears, transfixed by their attachments and desires. They are unwilling to let go, to leave what they have known, to reclaim the pieces of themselves they have given away in this way.

It is a very difficult test, one which takes great courage and strength: to acknowledge your fears and the creations of your life and reclaim from them your soul. Some, too afraid to relinquish a corporeal form, become frantic to recapture their Earthly existence, and so reincarnate before they have had time to absorb the lessons of the life they have most recently left.

Not only do these souls postpone by this choice the experience of indescribable freedom and infinite love that awaits them, they also create even greater difficulties and challenges for themselves by going back, when their spirits are ready to progress to the next level of learning and development.

Others, refusing to let go, paralyzed by their fear, are trapped here in this limbo world, until they are awakened from their illusion. Yet, the universe has not abandoned them. For I also could feel in this space the myriad prayers offered up by those still living for the safe passage of these souls. The overwhelming power of prayer, as well as the presence of many enlightened ones sent to help free trapped spirits from the bonds of their attachments, forms a great mirror in which they may finally see the truth of their enslavement. Only then will they be able to move away from confusion and death toward eternity.

As I passed through this challenging space, I kept my heart open and my whole being focused on the Great Love that lies beyond all illusion. I did not refuse my lessons, nor did I allow myself to be pulled by my fears or my Earthly memories from this bright core of molten love. Of my own volition, and with the support and encouragement of my beloved spirit guide, I cast the last remaining chains that bound me to my Earthly existence into this sacred furnace of flaming Love.

The illusion of this testing ground then shattered into a thousand, thousand pieces, and we were once again traveling unimpeded through an endless space of light and indescribable harmonies. We passed through many levels, within them great and beautiful gardens, and lovely temples of light, filled with many voices — all rejoicing. At each level, I was asked if I desired to stay, to experience what that existence held for me. I had at one time or another participated in all of these Heaven Worlds; and although they each possessed their own unique gifts, their own particular beauty and truths, I had already made those a part of my being and grown from them as a soul. There was no need for me there, and so my spirit flew on through the light.

I then reached a great endless field of moving color and immense living sound. This was where I had been headed all along; this was where I truly belonged. I was no longer "I" alone; I was now "I" in everything.

To describe this place to you is impossible. It is made up of the pure and all-encompassing and mighty power of Love. It is everywhere. It is nonconfining. It is nonlimiting. It is total surrender. It is melting in ecstatic union with the Divine. It is greater than any loving union you will ever experience in human form. Here, you retain your awareness and your ability to feel, yet you have surrendered all illusion of separation. There is no more "you" or "I" . . . there is only us.

After an endless time spent in this sacred bliss, I began to feel a pull at the very center of my essence. This pull was the manifestation of a need the universe had, which only I could satisfy. A living cord of light formed that connected me to the source of that need. I let myself be carried by that cord back through endless levels of light to a Heaven World that is much closer to the Earth. As I drew nearer to my destination, I felt my energy condense, until I was once again wearing the form familiar to me at this level. I found myself walking in a Heavenly garden, surrounded by spirit beings and beautiful souls filled with light and celebration.

I knew I would find here one who needed something only I could provide: healing through forgiveness. I had forgiven him long, long ago, And though he had been told the truth of this many times, in many ways, he needed to experience forgiveness directly. He needed the mirror of my forgiveness to see clearly his great goodness and to accept the truth of this.

This man, Michael, this incomparable soul, is my beloved, my brother. I treasure him beyond all measure. I honor his courage and his purity of spirit. He was finally able to see who he really is reflected in my eyes. This man, who saw himself as my destroyer, was then able to accept the truth of the beauty and healing that he, through his choices, created from that destruction. This vision finally freed him. He is now able to surrender fully to the love of the universe, to accept the path of mercy and wonder held out to him.

We are all ultimately responsible for the welfare of every other soul. We are all connected at the deepest level of our being, and if one of us falls we will all ultimately suffer. If one of us flies free, then we will feel that, too. We are one holy family, bound together forever by a union of spirit. Nothing born of Love can ever die. The universe has grown out of and rests on this truth. You, too, can rest in the unchanging truth of this forever.

Look for me in the rainbow. Listen for my voice in the joyous song of the bird. I live in your heart, and you in mine. This is the unchanging law of the Divine, which knows only ultimate union and unending Love.

The angels said of Michael and Li, "Forgiveness is the beginning of all healing. It is the source of true freedom and enlightenment. Without total forgiveness of self and others, there can never be the complete immersion of a soul in Love."

16

Cultivating Forgiveness

The need for forgiveness is a theme that recurs again and again in my work with people intent on improving their lives, whether it is on an emotional, spiritual, or physical level.

Most healers, from whatever culture, stress the importance of this concept as a necessary ingredient in creating a balanced life. The kahuna, priests of Huna, the religion indigenous to the Hawaiian Islands, teach that all disease—whether mental, physical, or spiritual—has at its source the inability to forgive oneself or another.

This refusal to embrace a path of forgiveness creates a constriction on all levels, inhibiting the free flow of the life force, with its regenerative, healing properties. The inability to forgive creates obstacles to receiving the gifts that life's lessons have to offer us: an expanded compassion and the ability to love unconditionally.

According to our heavenly teachers, these two qualities allow us to transcend our belief in separation—from the Earth, from each other, from God. Their promise is that "this transcendence can only lead to the ultimate ecstatic experience of true union, expanded awareness, and unlimited freedom."

The first step in the journey to forgiveness starts with willingness. Many, like Michael, are unable to accept the possibility that they could be worthy of absolution. Others will fight like tigers for the right to bear an unending grudge, to exact vengeance from those they perceive as having wronged them.

Both are unwittingly arguing with all their might to remain victims of past dramas. They thus perpetuate these dramas ad infinitum. In this way, though they may appear to assume the stance of warrior, well armed with self-righteousness, or that of martyr clothed in a hair shirt woven of self-pity and shame, they are in fact still victims. Much of their life force is bound up in arguing for this reality of pain. Thus, they seriously limit the energy that is available to them for growth, for healing, for giving and receiving love.

Because of their inability to surrender their rigid positions, they are unable to take back their power from these dramas, which many times exist in the mind only. In this way, they deny their role as true warriors possessing the strength and wisdom to create healing and balance in their souls and on this planet.

If you can accept that forgiving does not mean forgetting—that forgiving yourself or another does not mean you are condoning an action that may have caused great harm to yourself or to others— then it becomes easier to surrender to this process. It is the path that will lead you to the only true release of your pain.

It would, in many instances, be foolish to try to forget the actions that created the situations now causing us pain. The angels continually emphasize the wisdom of recognizing an inappropriate action. They encourage us to do everything in our power to right these wrongs, to prevent them from occurring again, to ourselves or to others. Our life experiences are to be learned from, not denied. However, too many times we get stuck in the lesson, repeating it over and over until it becomes a part of our false identity.

To condemn the perpetrator of an action that you perceive as wrong is not so appropriate. This creates a shadow, which obscures the power and glory of our true selves. We have an infinite capacity to take any situation, no matter how horrendous, and learn from it. In this way we heal and grow in spirit. Michael and Li beautifully demonstrated the power of this forgiveness path.

Life is not easy. For some, it is an excruciating experience. We have all made unwise decisions; some out of ignorance, others out of pain and fear. Deep down, even the most hardened criminal is starving for the same thing that motivates the innocent baby: love and acceptance.

Hatred, vengence, guilt, and self-condemnation are toxic emotions which feed on the inability to forgive. They weaken body, mind, and soul. Love strengthens; it heals and makes you whole. To prove this to yourself, take a moment to go within. Think of someone, or some situation, that you have not been able or willing to forgive. Feel the heaviness of this, the contracted tension, the darkness. Now, move your focus to someone or something you feel great love for. Allow yourself to experience the warmth, the elation, the calm peace you find there. If you had a choice—and you do— which place would you rather be in?

Once you recognize the need for forgiveness and you are willing, what then? It is relatively easy to embrace this concept on an intellectual level. It is one thing to say, "I forgive you," or "I forgive myself." It is another thing altogether to allow these words to come to live in your heart. Yet it is only there that forgiveness has the power to make you whole, to wash you clean, to complete your healing at the deepest level.

All forms of forgiveness, the angels are quick to point out, begin with clarity. Clarity eventually leads to understanding, which, in turn, allows the flower of compassion to bloom. If well tended, it's rare and delicate petals will then open to reveal unconditional Love.

So, for forgiveness to become a reality, you must first cultivate clarity. You must take action at a physical level to move your intent from the intellectual realm into this world. Following are some suggestions to help facilitate this process.

If your task is forgiveness of self, you could start by making a list of all the possible reasons which might have led to the action that you are finding it difficult to release. Go back as far as you can remember into your childhood memories, for inappropriate actions are often caused by unconscious fears or pain with roots buried deep in past experiences.

Pretend that you are viewing these memories from outside of yourself, as if you were watching a movie. The point of this is to disengage at an emotional level, so that you can begin to see things more objectively, and therefore, more clearly. What part of these circumstances was within your capacity to control, and what part was not?

Now look at how you might have done things differently, how you could have handled your pain or anger differently. What were you really trying to accomplish with that action? How can you achieve this in a more appropriate manner in the future? How can you be more aware of, and therefore more responsible for, the effects of your actions on others? What characteristics do you need to nurture in yourself to allow this to happen?

If the person you feel you have wronged is available, and it would not cause further harm, go to them and take responsibility for your inappropriate actions. (If you feel it is more appropriate, you may choose to write them a letter.) Acknowledge their pain, and ask their forgiveness for being the cause of their suffering. Ask if there is anything you can do to help them, to heal any damage you might have done. Then, if their request is in alignment with the good of the whole, if it will promote peace and healing, do everything you can to comply with their wishes. The angels acknowledge the fact that "this takes great courage, but the rewards are beyond price."

If it is not possible or appropriate to communicate directly with them, you can write out your thoughts. The purpose of writing these thoughts down is not to deliver them. Rather, it serves as your statement of intent. It declares your desire to create a healing in this situation. By writing down your thoughts and feelings, you move them out of the darkness of your subconscious and into the light of this reality.

Then pick a quiet time and place where you will not be disturbed, and visualize this person whom you feel you have wronged. When you can see and feel them clearly, address them, saying to them all the things you would were they available to you. Because we are all connected, on some level they will sense this communication, especially if it is backed with the true emotion of the heart. You can ask the angels to help you with this, to carry your message to its intended receiver.

Finally, identify the imbalance that your inappropriate actions may have created or helped to perpetuate in the world. Look around you. Is there something you can devote your time and energy to that would help to balance and heal this imbalance? For example, if your guilt stems from a failure to nurture your parents in their final years, you could volunteer time helping the elderly in your community, or you could promote or help to implement programs that will benefit them in some way.

Taking action releases you forever from the old patterns, which only cause stagnation of the spirit and the perpetuation of pain in the world. Rather than allowing your suffering to paralyze you, and prevent further soul growth, you will instead be utilizing it as impetus to create healing in yourself, and in the world. As Li expressed so eloquently to Michael, in showing love and caring for those around you, you are loving the one who may, for whatever reason, not be able to receive that love in person.

The process of forgiving another can be accomplished in much the same way as forgiveness of the self. You can begin with making a list of all the possible scenarios that could have led that person to the inappropriate action, which hurt you or made you angry. If you do not know much about that person, use the power of your imagination, going back as far as you can into their past. It is important, as always, to use compassion, to give this person the benefit of the doubt. You would be surprised at how accurate some of these imagined events can be. Although we may sometimes seem very different, one from another, the angels are quick to remind us that we are all One at the deepest part of our being. We are more alike than we think we are!

Try to see and acknowledge the great pain or fear or ignorance that lies behind the hurtful action. Next, acknowledge any part you may have had in catalyzing the hurtful behavior that you are having a difficult time forgiving, and take responsibility for it. This may or may not apply to your particular situation.

Look for the ways this person and the events in question may be serving as a teacher for you. As the angels say, "All difficulties have at their center an invaluable gift for you, a lesson that will lead you to a greater wholeness of spirit. They reveal to you unacknowledged places of weakness in the soul. You have the capacity to shore them up and thus grow in strength and wisdom."

Acknowledge that, although you will no longer allow yourself to be subject to their inappropriate behavior, you are not rejecting this person as a spirit, born of the same universe, here to learn lessons, many the hard way! You may need to ask for God's help at this point to remove any resistance.

Surrender the self-imposed walls of protection around your heart that sometimes present themselves as hurt or rage. Acknowledge that love is the greatest protection. Love sees all and understands. It is this clarity and understanding that will prevent a recurrence of the situation which hurt you. You will gain an awareness of your true motives, as well as those of others. You will see the potential for harm coming long before it happens and be able to divert it before it has a chance to create another imbalance.

Armed with your new awareness and openness, go to the person you feel hurt you in some way. This action is to be taken only if you feel it would not create further damage, and you are certain that your motivation in doing so is to make peace rather than to cause harm. Tell them how their actions affected you, and why you felt they were inappropriate. *It is most important that you do not do this in an accusatory manner.*

Then, allow them to relate their interpretation of the event in question. You may need to remind yourself to stay open and really listen at this point. Listen beyond the words, which may be defensive or hurtful. In this way you will come to know the soul behind the personality, which may still be attached to the drama of the situation. After giving them time to tell their side of the story, in your own words say, "Although I am in no way open to repeating this experience, which caused me great hurt, I am now willing to let it go. I extend to you the olive branch of peace. I wish you only blessings in your life."

This does not mean you must take this person back into your life, or interact with them in any way in the future. Many times this is neither appropriate, nor is it possible. In closing, you may wish to present to them a peace offering, such as a flower, or something you have made and treasure. This declares to them as well as to your subconscious that you are serious. Whether they accept it or throw it back in your face, it will have benefited you as well as them. For somewhere inside all their pain, they will hear you. You have planted seeds, which will then have a chance to grow into an expanded heart.

If direct interaction with the person is for whatever reason not possible, you can write out all your thoughts and feelings, everything that you wish you could say. Then surrender it to God, let it go, by burning it, allowing the winds of heaven to disperse your intent throughout the universe, where it will reach the one you are forgiving at some level.

The process of forgiveness is never easy. It could be the greatest challenge you will face during your time on this planet. It may be necessary to devote days, weeks, even months, to this evolutionary act. Yet, in the end you will without question experience an undeniable expansion of heart, a lightness of spirit, and a mighty empowerment at all levels. You will feel the whole universe smiling!

17

The Stories of Possessing Spirits and Those They Possess

*A*s the stories of Ruth and David revealed, events do not always unfold smoothly during the transition known as death. We now found ourselves exposed to the more turbulent waters on the other side, and to the possible experiences of those awaiting souls who, because of fear or self-judgment, choose to fight the great river of Love that carries us Home.

On a bright day in early spring, as Helen and I settled into our normal places to begin the session, I immediately sensed that something was different. As always, there appeared a great angel of brightness. His presence filled the room with an intensity that loosened the hold of this reality on my mind and body, allowing me to glimpse an expanded view of existence. Within this Light I felt a small whirlwind of darker, heavier energy—chaotic and dissimilar to anything we had confronted in our explorations up to now.

As I penetrated deeper into this chaotic whirlwind, I could sense two distinct souls—one male, one female. Both were totally absorbed in themselves. Their energies, rather than radiating out, seemed to implode, creating two black holes with the capability of absorbing all the light around them.

Because of the choices these beings made during their lives, at the time of their deaths they became trapped in that space between worlds and are now what you would term *ghosts*. They are angry and confused. They still carry addictions that they have had for many lifetimes, therefore they cannot proceed along the path down which their spirit wishes to carry them. In this sense they have turned their backs on God.

In their great anguish and confusion and despair, they create chaos on this planet. One way in which they do this is by attaching themselves to the living. Through this attachment they are capable of creating great discomfort and difficult challenges for those whom they possess. If this is a human who has an addiction shared by the disembodied spirit, then the addictive tendencies and dysfunctional behaviors of that human will be greatly magnified.

The angel assured us that we were protected from these souls. Rather than speaking directly to them, their stories would instead be relayed to me through the angel. He would give to me information about and visions of their lives and deaths and present realities as disembodied spirits. The following is an account of what I saw and experienced during this time.

The angel is here and he has brought two people with him — a man and a woman. These souls have become what is known as possessing spirits. They are souls of humans who have been trapped in the space between worlds by their Earthly attachments, or addictions. Their attachment to these addictions has swallowed them up, usurped their will. The need to satisfy their obsession has become greater than their need for anything else. It has become God to them.

Many people, at some point during their lives, experience a deep hole, an aching emptiness at the core of their being. This ache is a longing for union with God and is experienced when a soul, for whatever reason, loses touch with the knowing that it is forever one with the Divine, never truly separate from the whole. Rather than seeking to fill that emptiness by losing the self in love for God, love for the Earth, love for another as God loves — unconditionally, without expectation — which is the door to being filled in turn with the soothing balm of God's love, they choose instead to attempt to assuage their pain through selfish love.

Selfish love focuses on the self and on the gratification of the urges and desires of that self with total disregard to the effect of these actions on the whole. Instead of facing their discomfort and pain as a warrior—finding the imbalances causing the disconnection from the whole, and then healing those imbalances through the light of understanding and compassion—they choose to numb their discomfort and run away from the pain. The source of that self-gratification and escape then becomes of paramount importance to them. In every sense, it becomes God to them—the ruling force and sole motivator of their existence. They surrender their heart, their mind, their soul, to this thing without which they feel they cannot live.

Yet ironically, rather than bringing them closer to the healing, the connection for which they are searching, it takes them farther and farther away. It blinds the soul to the truth of its power and origins and serves to build a wall between that soul and the whole, between that soul and its true source of strength and well-being.

So it is in the case of these two souls. They surrendered their will to addictions while they were alive. At the time of their death, these addictions had become the greatest power, the only reality to them. They surrendered so totally to their obsessions that those obsessions controlled every aspect of their existence. Every action, every decision was predicated upon the satisfaction of these needs. Their addictions, at this point, have penetrated beyond the physical, beyond even the emotional level, to live in their souls.

Their reluctance to release their addictions and to face themselves and their reality as warriors, their inability to trust in the love and infinite mercy of God, keeps them trapped in a gray limbo space. This is a nightmare reality of confusion, anger, and devouring thirst for that which was all consuming to them in life—a thirst that will never be quenched, a lust for sensations that will never be satiated but only become more excruciatingly torturous.

Yet despite the suffering this creates for them, they continue to pursue the source of that suffering—even in death. They search out and find living individuals through which they can vicariously live out these addictions. Put simply, they attach themselves to those who have similar obsessions, merge with their energy field, and then do everything they can to encourage that person to continue their addictive behavior.

Because those humans being possessed have surrendered their will to addiction, it is very easy to persuade them to indulge their obsessions, to push them deeper and deeper into total enslavement to their destructive, devouring desires. The possessing spirits learn very quickly how best to do this. They have the ability to influence the thoughts and behavior of those made susceptible to them by similar obsessions. They grow adept at interjecting dreams and visions into the subconscious mind and inducing feelings and desires in the physical body.

Those being possessed can be influenced in this way because they have lost their spiritual immunity. They have weakened the link between themselves and God by ignoring the voice of the Divine that lives in us all, directing us along the path that will lead us back to our true selves. God never deserts us, but we can desert God. And so, by throwing away the map which directs their progress in a way that is best for them as well as for the whole, they allow themselves to be very easily misled.

These addictions also weaken their energy field—the light of the spirit that radiates from every being. This makes it very easy for a disembodied soul to attach itself to and sometimes even to penetrate and merge with the soul in the body, so that the human then takes on the characteristics, emotions, and personality of the disembodied soul.

In rare cases, what we know of as possession can occur in instances where those in a body have "disassociated" during times of extreme stress or trauma. In other words, rather than staying present in the body to deal with whatever situation in which it found itself, that soul chose to vacate the body for the duration of the event, leaving only a fragment behind to ensure the survival of the physical vehicle. During these times, a weakness in the integrity of the energy field is created, which can allow for penetration and possession of the body by a disembodied soul. Afterward, the person in the body finds that they now may experience feelings, thoughts, and urges they never had before.

In the case of these two souls, the humans that they have chosen to possess share the same addictions as they, and this is what has made those humans susceptible to possession.

The first of these disembodied souls is a woman known as Edith. She, as well as the male spirit—whose name, I am told, is Frank—has retained the physical form and personality that she had while she was living. She is very large, overweight, very lethargic, and unhealthy physically as well as emotionally. She has a dazed expression on her face, a glazed look in her eye, both of which reflect her soul sickness. The darkness of desperation and severe depression emanate from and surround her. She is heavy physically as well as emotionally.

Edith's addiction was to food and to the emotional state known as depression. Because of her inability to face the challenges that arose while she was living, she took on the identity of martyr and victim—an identity that further disempowered her to take responsibility for her actions and control of her life choices. She gave up and turned to the pleasures of food to fill the hole that self-hatred and bitterness had created in her soul. She attempted to sweeten that bitterness with chocolates and find love in ice cream and cakes, the rewards of her youth.

She is unable to release her harsh and unforgiving judgments of self and others. In life these judgments separated her from the realization of her oneness with all of creation. They prevented her from feeling God's Love and the love that others tried to show her. She alienated all of those in her life who attempted to draw close to her. In the end she died of heart failure at the age of thirty-nine—a direct result of closing her heart to giving and receiving love, choosing instead to attempt to numb her pain with food.

Immediately after leaving her body—despite all attempts made by her guardian angel to comfort and guide her to the experiences on the other side that will heal her deep wounds—

she attached herself to one who she sensed had the same tendencies toward overeating and depression. She has since been with this woman, whom we will call Pam, constantly. She does not possess Pam in that she enters into the physical body, but she does stay always merged with her energy field.

Since her possession by Edith, Pam's depression has deepened, her overeating has been greatly exacerbated. Depression creates a weakened energy field and lowers the vibrational frequency of the body to the point that many times the voice which holds the truth of that person's beauty and strength cannot penetrate the conscious mind. This state then feeds upon itself, creating an inertia that eventually affects the body at a physiological level, shutting down the parts of the brain capable of manifesting the higher vibrations of joy, passion, and hope, and diminishing the level of life force available to that person. Depression begins many times with the denial of a path that needs to be taken to fulfill a particular destiny, or with a fear of expressing the great creative force that is the very essence of our being. It can be balanced and healed by pushing past that fear to allow the soul to express its deepest need for creative manifestation.

Pam has a desire to change, to take control of her actions. Intellectually she knows what she must do. Yet during times of stress, she falls back into the old, familiar patterns of self-berating judgment, paranoia, and finding solace in food. These tendencies are encouraged and magnified by Edith's presence in her life. Since Edith joined her almost two years ago, these destructive patterns have become deeply entrenched and overwhelming. Edith will remain with Pam, living vicariously through her misery — perpetuating the state which is most familiar to her — until Pam overcomes her dependence upon and identification with addictive behaviors. Only when she finds the courage within herself to replace these old patterns of disempowerment with patterns that acknowledge her strength and beauty and worthiness — patterns which allow her to give and to receive love freely — will she close the door to Edith's influence.

When Pam does finally break the chains that are holding her soul back from its true manifestation, Edith will no longer have any power over her. Edith will then quickly find another through which to live out her obsessions. She could conceivably spend an eternity in this way. Yet, God never gives up on a soul. Her angel will remain with her to offer her a bright and shining, love-filled alternative to her present loveless gray existence.

At this point, however, Edith is overwhelmed by immense anxiety and terror when she considers leaving the Earthly realm of the senses. There she continues to attempt to assuage her pain by seeking to satisfy her unending hunger for love and acceptance through food. Yet deep in the cloud of grayness that Edith has become is a part of her that is screaming for love, screaming for help. The universe hears that cry. When she is ready to trust in the Love of God and surrender to that Love, she will then be able to find within her soul the power to release her obsession and turn, instead, to God for her sustenance.

Frank, too, has a little boy inside that is crying, but he cannot acknowledge this. He spent his whole life running away from that little boy's pain. He chose to hide from this pain in his addictions to alcohol, tobacco, and the sensations of lust. These things numbed his senses and his ability to experience anything but the lower vibrational frequencies, so that he became unable to feel love for others or to receive the love that was shown him. The only time he felt alive was through his experience of these lower frequencies. This living death became his whole identity. It was as a homeless addict in the throes of his addictions that he finally left this world, having destroyed his life and the lives of all those who cared for him through the blind and mindless pursuit of his obsessions.

After his death, his soul immediately found its way to the bar where he spent his last years on Earth. He would choose patrons of this establishment and follow them home. He did this several times until he found a man with precisely the right combination of addictions to suit him. We will call this man

Ed. Ed is addicted to pornography and prostitutes, cigarettes and gin — exactly those things to which Frank had turned for satisfaction and fulfillment.

Ever since Frank attached himself to Ed, Ed's addictions have totally consumed him. When he drinks he will drink until he blacks out. It is at this point that Frank can actually enter into and control Ed's body. During this process, Ed's soul is pushed into a dark corner of his being, imprisoned there by Frank's presence. Ed's soul sleeps and while it is sleeping, Frank does what he will with Ed's life.

Furthermore, Frank is not the only one who takes advantage of Ed's state. There are other disembodied souls — all trapped in that limbo space by similar obsessions — who literally fight over the opportunity to experience their addictions again, however briefly, through Ed's helpless body. While these souls are in possession of the body, that body takes on the memories, personality, and characteristics of the soul who is in control. These possessing souls will then vacate the body only when the sensations or circumstances that they have created become too perilous or too unpleasant. At that point, Ed returns to a life that has been muddied and a body that has been greatly damaged by souls run amok. Frank finds this very amusing.

Every time Ed drinks to the extent that he loses conscious awareness, he further weakens his energy field, making it that much simpler for Frank and others to take control of his body. If he does not reclaim his power by changing his addictive behaviors, they will eventually destroy him. This does not concern those souls who feed off of his habits. They have no affection for Ed, only contempt. They will simply find another through which to satisfy their needs once Ed's body is no longer viable.

The only way for Ed to regain control and rid himself of these errant souls, who are literally killing him, is to take his authority back from his addictions, reclaim his will, and give his allegiance back to God. God will continually create opportunities for Ed to do this. However, the choice to open himself to the healing light of the Divine must be his.

Frank's form reflects his soul sickness. He appears emaciated, colorless, lecherous, and unwell. The air around him is permeated by a convoluted, twisted, polluted feeling. Yet, there is still the child of innocence crying deep inside of all that sickness. That child holds Frank's true essence. This essence will eventually lead Frank to his salvation and freedom from the space where his addictions hold him captive. At the present time, however, he has turned his back on those angels who are there to help him. He is simply not interested. The only thing he is interested in is living out his obsessions vicariously through others who are still alive. He is aware that he is dead. He is also aware of the reality of a Heaven World, but he cannot imagine an existence without the objects of his desires. He knows that the only way for him to continue to have access to the sensations he craves is to stay where he is. He is unwilling at this time to leave.

Prayers for these lost souls and for those who are trapped by their addictions send a powerful energy to the object of those prayers. This energy has the capability of waking them up to the truth of their situation, regardless of whether they are still in a body or trapped in the space between worlds. Loving prayer filled with and strengthened by the authority of God can also free those possessed from the souls who possess them. Prayer will only be effective, however, if these individuals are willing to take responsibility for their lives and for balancing through right action the imbalances that their choices have created. Once they wake up and accept this responsibility, then they can begin to heal those things that prevent them from experiencing Heaven and the great and all-forgiving Love that God has for us.

18

xavier

*L*ate one night during the period I was receiving the information for this book, I was awakened by a beautiful angel of great light and strength. He informed me that he had brought with him one who "was once human but chose to turn his back on his Divinity." Through this angel I was to hear from a soul who resides in the place we know as Hell.

Listening to this man's story, witnessing how twisted a soul can become when it chooses a dark path, was excruciating. I was aware of a miasma of toxic emotions—lust, depravity, cruelty, and fear—emanating from this lost soul. Despite the protection of the mighty angel, I still became physically ill for several days. At times I questioned the inclusion of this material at all. My natural tendency is to protect those around me from the dark side of life. Yet I also realized that the story of this soul holds a great truth. Only if we are aware of the great imbalances held in the souls of men, as well as in the realities surrounding us, will we have the power to heal and balance the whole.

What you are about to read is extremely unpleasant, frightening, and graphic—presented just as it was presented to me. If you do not wish to experience this man's torturous life and his misery in death, turn to the next chapter.

*   *   *

My name is Xavier. I grew up on the streets of Rio, in Brazil. I last walked those streets in the third week of October, 1983. I died in those streets with a needle in my arm. I was nineteen.

I do not know who my father was. Neither did my mother. She was a whore. As a child I spent most of my time on the streets or in the whore's bedroom. When I was four, the whore began to sell me to the men, too. I liked the attention and the little gifts they would bring me. My mother was very young and darkly seductive. I never knew any other family. She never spoke of parents or brothers or sisters, aunts or uncles. Our family was the men and the drugs and the "magic" woman who lived two doors down the alley—old Juanita.

Many days and nights we never left that room. The men never stopped knocking at the door. Sometimes they brought money, sometimes food, sometimes drugs. I grew to like the feelings in my body that these men could arouse. These feelings were the only ones I knew, and I liked it that way. I preferred the men who hurt the whore with whips and chains and bottles. I really liked that feeling, too—hurting and being hurt. It enhanced the lust and I loved the lust, I became lust. I couldn't get enough—the drugs and the frenzied lust.

I would go with the whore every Saturday evening and every full moon to Juanita's. There would be others there, too. The first time I was taken there I was three. There were candles burning and another child—a girl who was only an infant. I remember she wouldn't stop crying. I do not know where she came from.

They put her in the middle of the floor and the others gathered around her and Juanita began to speak in a singsong way. I didn't understand the words but they lulled me into a state where I could not move. Then Juanita entered the circle and raised her silver dagger over the child and the crying stopped; in the silence that followed, I felt the dark power that comes with the death of innocence.

A man brought in a rabbit. He gave me a knife and made

me slit its throat and drink its blood. I felt important and excited. That was my initiation into the Devil's family — the only family that ever totally accepted me. Whatever in me might have chosen goodness and compassion died that night with the rabbit and the girl child.

When I was thirteen, I began to go into the streets to find more stimulation. I got this by luring young girls and boys with my beauty and my magic into dark corners where I would rape, torture, and finally kill them. Many times I would find the sacrifices for Juanita. I would drug these beautiful, fresh, young children and bring them to the ceremonies where there was always torture and sex. I lived for this and for the dark power that filled me during these times. When I wasn't having sex for money, or raping, I was stimulating myself or doing drugs or killing animals. It gave me pleasure and a deep sense of power to watch them die.

I learned how to allow other spirits into my body so that they, too, could experience these things. I was aware of their presence around me always and was taught at Juanita's how to use them to do my bidding. If I was angry, I could send them to hurt and create terror. If I wanted to lure an innocent girl or boy to a place where I could trap them and then enjoy their slow suffering and terror, I could send the demons to create a lust in these helpless victims. The more innocent and filled with goodness these children were, the greater was my pleasure. My world was a dark place. I was born into it and I died in it. I am not like others. God didn't want me but the Devil does. He gives me power and purpose. Without him I am nothing — without the lust I cannot exist.

When I died — from bad smack — I saw myself in the street, lying in a crumpled heap. I looked around and saw the demons of darkness who had been with me forever, but now they were joined by a great being of light. I remembered him from when I was a very young child, before the demons came. I was not afraid of him as a child, but now I was terrified of this thing, which must be an angel. I still am afraid. I cannot look too closely at him or I am paralyzed with fear.

The angel was trying to get me to listen to him. He was telling me to follow him into the Light — that he loved me, God loved me. He said that, even though my actions had created great harm and could not be condoned by God, I was not rejected by Him, but was forgiven. A way would be made for me to make up for all I had done. Meanwhile, the spirits of darkness, who had been with me and served me well, were doing their best to distract me and lure me away from this light by filling my consciousness with visions of depravity. These visions stirred an intense hunger in me which overrode any fear or confusion as to what I was to do.

This dark hunger pulled me like a whirlpool down into a place that was filled with many souls screaming and crying and laughing — madly laughing. The sound was deafening and discordant. There I found all the depravity I was promised and more.

After a time, I began to feel a deep inertia and a growing despair. I became aware, in the depths of my soul, of pain and a longing for something more. I could see at the edge of this swirling place of darkness a large group of angels. They never left that space to come into the darkness, but I could feel them calling to me. They still call but I cannot go with them. I am not of their kind. I am nothing without the Devil and his family. If I do leave here and go with the angels, I will burn up in the Light. And I know I cannot exist without the lust. Yet something keeps calling me. I want to believe what they are saying, but I cannot leave here to go with them. This is my place.

Sometimes I am drawn to the space between your world and ours by humans whose actions feed my need for lust. I can experience through them the way this felt as a human. It is somewhat different, yet the same. I feel pleasure in adding to the corruption of innocence, by fueling dark fantasies in this human — aided by those demons who never leave my side — and then by pushing him to act on those fantasies. Humans who are addicted to power or drugs or alcohol or sex are the easiest to influence. I am rewarded greatly for this, in the place known as Hell, with more power. Yet the gaping hole in my soul is screaming louder each day, and I am a prisoner of my dark desires and the fears of a weak spirit. I cannot leave here. This is the only place where they will accept me. I have power here. . . . So why does my soul cry? I never cried as a human. So why now does my soul cry?

The angel who was with Xavier then explained more of why Xavier had become a fallen soul.

Xavier, by his choices in life and after his death, has lowered his vibrational essence and trapped himself in the pit. During his life, although he had many difficult challenges, he was constantly confronted with the potential for goodness in himself by the innocence and goodness of those he used and destroyed. Yet, because of self-judgment, he sees himself as different from others, beyond redemption. I have been here for him since the beginning of this journey, to reflect to him his potential for goodness and to offer him God's Love and forgiveness and healing. But he must first let go of his dark obsessions and choose to turn his face toward God. He must forgive himself and give his soul the opportunity to once again know God and, through that knowing, find the courage to atone for his actions.

Until that time, I am here, hand outstretched at the edge of darkness. When the longing and despair in his soul become greater than his fear, he will take my hand and his journey back to Love will begin. This is not an easy journey. It will take much hard work and courage, but there is overwhelming love and compassion and forgiveness to help him over the rough spots. In this way he may once again reclaim the destiny that God deemed appropriate for us all in the beginning — one of Love and Celebration and Joyous Creation.

19

Evil, Demons, and Hell

*W*hat exactly is Hell? What are demons? Did God create them? If not, where did they come from and what, if anything, can we do about them?

The idea of demons and the existence of Hell are extremely frightening to the majority of people—so much so that many of them absolutely deny the reality of evil. Others live their entire lives in terror of being consigned to the "fiery pit," at the mercy of horrific and cruel demonic beings. Their every action is motivated not by love and compassion, but by an abject fear of this hapless state. They see Satan behind every bush. The Devil becomes more real to them than their distant God, who, in their belief system, is not merciful, but vengeful and punishing and unforgiving. This fearful existence creates a suspicious rather than a trusting nature, judgment rather than compassionate understanding, and a contracted rather than an open and expansive heart.

This is what the angels have to say on the subject.

Evil is contraction. Evil rejects. Goodness forgives and accepts. Divine consciousness sees beyond evil to the source of the contraction, to the source of the pain and the choices made as the result of that pain, which led to the creation of evil by a soul. The Divine, while not accepting the inappropriate actions of a soul, can nevertheless love and forgive that soul in spite of its choices. Evil is a movement away from God, destructive to all life. Goodness is a movement toward God, supportive of all life. These diverse movements are fueled by the same energy that originates at the fountainhead of the Divine. Yet, the end results of these choices are very different — one destroys the soul's strength and integrity, while the other empowers and enlightens the soul. So man, by his choices, molds this God-given energy into different experiences. Therefore, it is man who is primarily responsible for and ultimately the source of evil.

In the beginning, the souls of humans were given the gift of free will. They were made co-creators with God. This gift included the ability to make decisions that directly affect the shape and form of reality. The effects of these decisions are not confined to one level of existence; they ultimately touch all levels of Creation, for humans are very powerful beings. Their thoughts contain a force that creates — not only at the level of physical existence, but at other levels as well — the very thing upon which they focus. Where your energy is placed, where your thought is placed and then backed by emotion, there will your reality manifest, there will you realize the fruit of your creative labors.

When the thoughts and emotions of man are focused at the lower vibratory frequencies associated with greed, lust, cruelty, hatred — any experience that negates love — these thoughts and emotions then become the genesis point for most demonic energy. A demonic being is any individualized essence that has as its motivating force the destruction of the soul and the turning of that soul away from the Divine, away from its oneness with the whole. Because these beings were created not by God, but by the contracted energies emanating from the hearts of men, they are soulless entities. They were formed of and are perpetuated and fed by the collective darkness emanating from the minds and emotions of souls who have rejected their true essence.

Many of these demons have been deliberately called into being by humans who turn their backs on the one source of

true power and fulfillment—a total surrender to the Divine and
an acceptance of their deep connection to the whole of creation.
Rather than being filled with the love and peace that comes
with this acceptance of their true nature, they are instead filled
with fear and a deep aching emptiness over which they feel
powerless. The desperate need to relieve this experience of
helplessness renders them willing to do anything to control
their surroundings and those by whom they feel threatened.
Their fear drives them to create, by the calling up of lower
emotional energies, a demonic essence. They then enlist this
essence to do their bidding in an attempt to achieve power over
their reality.

These types of demonic beings, because they have no souls,
also have no knowing of God, of what is best for the whole.
They have no life force, no spiritual energy of their own, and
are therefore dependent for their existence upon the perpetuation and absorption of inappropriate energies generated by
human action and emotion. They become the very embodiment
of such emotions as lust, hatred, greed, fear, and cruelty. They
can easily be directed by humans bent upon the misuse of
power. These humans then become their masters for a time.
Yet, inevitably the master is overcome and destroyed by his
creation. This demonic being then moves on to create more
mindless destruction and chaos in the lives and souls of susceptible individuals.

The human creators of these demons are the true source of
evil. They have turned their backs on the gifts that God gave
them and on their rightful place in the universe. They have
turned their backs on love. Their only goal is power. This need
to control all they see and to destroy what they cannot control
stems from a deep fear. That fear is the fear of not being a
part of—not being loved, not being cared for or nurtured, not
safe in God's arms. This fear is no longer simply a feeling—it
has become a reality for these souls who believe they are separate and very, very alone in a hostile universe.

This is what these lost souls experience. This is what they
live. This is not God's reality, but the reality they have created

for themselves. And because this reality is devoid of love and nurturing, peace or acceptance, they feel an overwhelming need to manipulate and control their external surroundings, in a vain attempt to gain something that ultimately will only be found by opening their hearts to love. They consciously or unconsciously call upon demonic beings, who were formed by the generation of lower energies and the pulling together of these energies over centuries, over aeons of time, in the hope that this will give them the power they seek. Instead, it leads only to more pain for them as individuals and the perpetuation of the presence of evil in the whole.

There also exist souls, who were created by God pure and filled with light, but who have chosen to manifest darkness. These souls were once balanced and whole. They have evolved at other levels of reality than the one in which you find yourselves. Because they chose to deliberately and willfully work against the good of the whole, they have become demonic. They have, by their actions, excluded themselves from the plan laid out for them by the Divine and entered into an existence of chaos and endless pain. Their only aim is destruction. This need to destroy comes from a wounded heart filled with despair. They have rejected love and contracted into a space of fear so deep and overwhelming that they no longer remember who they really are. These demonic beings are jealous of and bent upon destroying that which they have forgotten they themselves have. When they see someone who is filled with innocence and light, who would serve the good of the whole, it then becomes their sole intent to annihilate that goodness. If they cannot find an opening within the energy field of a light-filled human, they search out someone close by who possesses certain vulnerabilities. They then manipulate that vulnerable human to create discomfort and pain for the person of light, in the hopes that these challenges will cause them to turn away from their Divine source. They feel that if they can destroy all the Love in the universe, then they will no longer be reminded of that which they believe is lost to them forever, and their endless pain will cease.

These demons are vortexes of darkness, black holes in God's spiritual universe—the antithesis of light and love. Their aim is mindless destruction of all goodness, the extinguishing of God's Love in the hearts of all humans. For this love is the true Light of all Creation. They do everything in their power to encourage in susceptible individuals the darker emotions and desires, the inappropriate destructive behavior that leads to the lowering of the vibrational frequency of the soul. This contraction of energy then reduces the level of love and light which can manifest in the hearts of humans and, consequently, in this reality.

Man is most susceptible to manipulation and control at the level of the intellect. Therefore, these demons watch for an opportunity to influence the thoughts of an individual and then to create a separation between the intellect of that individual and the Divine Truth held within every heart. That individual then begins to act, not from a space of love where the effects of his actions on the good of the whole are considered, but only from a place of selfish motivation and the gratification of destructive, dark desires.

This susceptibility is heightened by addictions of all kinds, in that man in these instances begins to look to a source other than the Divine as the primary origin of his well-being. This creates a separation between his consciousness and the guidance and love of the Divine. He is no longer able to feel this constant love and begins instead to feel abandoned by the universe, afraid, lonely, self-judgmental. He begins to believe in and argue for his weaknesses rather than the innate strengths of the spirit. Demonic beings sense these weaknesses and will exploit them as openings to influence the addicted souls to fall even deeper into the living death of addiction. Some humans are so convinced of God's rejection and their powerlessness that they consciously and willingly invite these demons to dwell in their souls and influence and guide their lives in the mistaken belief that this will bring them fulfillment. Instead, it leads only to their destruction.

Humans who—through their addictions or practice of the

black arts or through the identification with lower emotions such as lust, self-hatred, cruelty, or greed — pull demonic energies into their reality will pass through a veil filled with these entities when they die. If they are unwilling to let go of their attachments to an identification with these emotions and move through this veil, they could be trapped there indefinitely. However, they will have the help of loving angels of light to guide them during this perilous time. If they but turn their face toward these angels in trust, then the messengers of God will help them to take the next step in healing their souls and in freeing themselves from the nightmare of darkness so that they may move toward the Light of the Divine.

Demons can ultimately lead a soul closer to its divinity, its enlightenment, by inadvertently pointing out through their interactions those weak places in the soul that need to be strengthened and shored up. These weaknesses are the result of unowned God-given strengths that the spirit has not yet recognized and incorporated. For in the end, demons, as terrifying and powerful as they can be, are nothing compared to the immense force of God's Love.

And what of Hell? Hell is not a place that was created by God. It is a space of great chaos and pain and terror and madness created by the beings who have chosen — whether consciously or unconsciously — to inhabit it. It came into being when these entities elected to negate and reject God's Love and His Divine Plan. Those who are drawn to this space are pulled there by their self-hatred. This self-hatred is the result of the surrender of the soul to fear, greed, lust, gluttony, cruelty, hate — to any emotion that is generated by a chosen action devoid of love. These emotions create a lowering of the vibrational frequencies of these souls, a darkening of their light. They then gravitate to a place that feels familiar to them — in this case, the space known as Hell, or the Underworld — which is filled with these darker emotions and with those who feed off of, identify with, and are made up of this darkness. Because of their self-judgment and rejection of God, they have closed their hearts. As long as their hearts are closed to the Love of

God, this dense barrier of despair and depravity and darkness remains impenetrable.

When a soul dies filled with self-loathing and judgment and a belief that God could not possibly love them or forgive them—that they must suffer for what they have done—these thoughts can eventually carry them into the Underworld. Those who die in the depths of addiction can also be drawn to this space, where those emotions and sensations to which they were addicted run rampant.

Some souls who occupy this hell-space were once human but have grown so far from God and so fearful of His retribution, so certain of harsh judgment, and so rejecting of their own beauty and worth that they feel this is their only true place. There they join forces with these demonic energies.

Hell exists at a different, chaotic vibrational frequency and is therefore separated from the whole by the belief constructs of those beings who inhabit it, who have created it by their rejection of the Divine. However, God has not rejected, nor has He abandoned them. Angels of great light surround this space—this black hole devoid of love. They stand at the edge of this deep darkness, ready at the slightest sign of repentance in a soul, to pull that soul into the light; here the soul may begin the work that will lead to its own healing and to the balancing of the imbalance that it, in its ignorance, has created in the whole. When these souls can forgive themselves and accept fully the love and forgiveness of God, when they find the courage to reach out—in that moment they are redeemed and freed.

Hell is the primary residing place of demonic beings—some soulless creations of man, some who of their own choice surrendered their soul's light to be engulfed in dark depravity. They feed off of the lower emotions that predominate there. They may leave this space when they are called up by human actions, but once they have completed their task, they return, for they cannot find the soul darkness that sustains them elsewhere—other than in the minds and souls of humans.

The war between good and evil, between the angels of

Heaven and demons from Hell in your legends and myths, is not simply an allegory for the struggle within each soul for balance between polarities. As within, so without. It is, therefore, on another level a very real physical battle between entities for the souls of humans.

This battle will ultimately be "won" by God, for the Divine is the source of all Creation, this great Love the beginning and the end. The farther away one travels from the source, the greater will be the pain and the pull back to that Center of all existence. The more a soul resists this pull, the greater will be its suffering. Eventually, all souls will return to God's Love, all lower emotions and the demonic entities who are the dark children of these emotions will be transmuted, healed, and integrated back into the whole. This will only happen when the mind and the body and the soul of man release all attachment to these energy constructs.

This release can happen through prayer for the surrender of the individual will to God's greater wisdom. This allows for Divine intervention and is the beginning of an existence ruled by Grace. This Grace lifts the soul and gives it wings to fly free of old patterns, unfettered by fear or resistance, back to the heart of God, its true and only home.

Prayer can call the great angels to do battle with the legions of darkness and to lift lost souls into the light of understanding and love. It opens the doors of the heart to receive the help of the universe, which is readily available to one who asks in faith. The prayer we speak of is not simply words learned by rote and repeated in a mindless fashion. Although it may take a verbal form, the essence of true prayer is beyond words. It is emotion and deep feeling and a great and overwhelming longing for and crying out to God. When this prayerful power is focused, it can bring about the fulfillment of a desire that has as its aim the benefit of the good of the whole by creating balance in the life of a person or an event.

It is not the words that are heard by the Divine Ear, but rather the emotions and feelings of sincerity and humility and power and love. These prayers echo thunderously through the heavens to touch the farthest reaches of the universe. There is no prayer, when it is backed by pure emotion, that is not heard and answered. Whenever a prayer is seemingly not answered, it is because the answer which was given is not one which was expected; therefore, it goes unrecognized.

Prayer opens up a direct connection between your world and the whole of creation. Prayer, when it is coupled with great impassioned love, is the most powerful force for change and healing and transformation in the universe. Many humans have forgotten how to pray in this way. They have lost touch with the ability to surrender to that wordless space of boundless feeling at the center of their being, which is the very heart and true essence of who they are. Reconnecting with that sacred place of power and then allowing it to radiate out from the heart in the focused form of prayer is the way to conscious co-creation with God. Creation then becomes an act of conscious love rather than the unconscious action of those who choose to live ruled by the inappropriate belief constructs of a sleeping, irresponsible soul.

Prayer can lift those in darkness into the light of understanding, forgiveness, and love. Pray for your enemy, for those whom you fear or fear for. Your prayers can heal the whole of Creation.

20

The Evolution of the Death Experience

The First Stories—origination myths found in all cultures—tell of a timeless time in the beginning when we walked the Earth in ageless, eternal bodies. We lived then in a land of endless bounty, of great wonder and beauty and peace, at one with each other, at one with all Creation.

What happened to change this idyllic existence? How did we fall away from God's perfect plan—fall away so far that we now find ourselves seemingly trapped in a narrowed prison: a reality filled with pain and separation, with suffering and death. We are spirit birds caught in a cage of limiting beliefs. Our freedom lies just beyond the bars of this cage. How do we escape so that we may once again fly free into the limitless horizon of possibility?

The angels offer the following information on the past and future of the human experience.

The specific reality in which you now find yourselves began as a coalescing of light into form, propelled by the thought of the Divine. This Light, which is the essence of all that is, was molded by the Mind of the Creator into a beautiful Paradise — a level of existence where the soul could experience itself as an individuated part of the whole. In the beginning, souls who chose to walk in this Paradise manifested fully formed. They could move easily from one reality into another by focusing their awareness — their thought — at a particular frequency. Their bodies were more fluid, much less dense than the ones that you now possess.

A soul would stay in this perfect world — playing, celebrating its awareness, creating and loving all of its creations — until it felt a need to leave this place for another realm. This need was the result of a greater need — generated at the Center of Creation — for this particular soul's presence and unique abilities at another level of existence, in order for the whole to maintain its perfect balance and harmony and form. That soul would then raise or lower its vibrational frequency — thus speeding up or slowing down the molecular structure of its shining form — until it left this space to join with another reality, where it would continue its evolution. For your true essence is fluid light — ever changing, ever responsive to the movement of the whole.

There was no point in this beginning time where the soul was not aware of its oneness with the whole, or of its responsibility and power as a co-creator with the Divine. Every soul used this power wisely. Through the empowerment of their thoughts with the energy of love and a will whose only intent was a pure and clear desire to serve and enhance the whole, they called into being a myriad kaleidoscope of changing form and experience. Every soul was a willing, perfectly accomplished member of a great celestial orchestra conducted by the Divine, merging their unique gifts and abilities to create a magnificent, ecstatic, ever-changing reality.

Then there came a time when some souls began to be so immersed in their experiences that they forgot their true nature. They became so focused on what they were creating that they closed out of their awareness their larger place in the whole. They then became attached to this narrowed focus and the creations contained within that focus. This attachment, along with the judgment that accompanies it, created a contraction within the souls. Attachment — to a particular place, a particular form, a particular experience or way of being — because of a judgment that one place was better than another, one form better than another, one experience or way of being better than another, began a slowing down of the vibrational frequency of the soul and, consequently, of the manifestations of that soul. Those things that were resisted, rejected out of judgment, began to be seen as separate. Out of this grew a belief that we were separate, one from another, separate from the Earth, separate from God.

When the time then came for a soul to let go of a particular manifestation in order to continue its evolution in a form or a place that would best benefit the whole, there was great reluctance. The soul began to reject the very essence of the spirit — which is ever-changing fluid light — in favor of an existence that was more rigid and resistant to change. This desire for stasis further slowed the vibration of the body — which is but an outgrowth of the desire of the soul for self-expression — to the point that it was no longer able to move freely between worlds.

However, because the spirit's existence is fluid light — ever growing toward more light — it cannot remain static. Therefore, out of the desires of a contracted soul was created the need for birth and death of the physical body in your world. When spirit found itself entrapped in a body whose soul personality refused to surrender to the changes necessary for growth, refused to let go of its attachments, its judgments — it then separated from the physical body so that soul could be free to re-create a situation more conducive to its continued evolution.

This necessitated the encoding into the DNA structure of every living thing the experience of the death of the body. In this way the spirit could ensure its continued growth in accordance with the Divine, from which it is never separate. The part that remained behind — that corporeal shell that had housed the soul and was encoded with contracted beliefs — was then transmuted, broken down so that it could become one with the reality to which it had created an attachment.

And Paradise — that Earthly place of such beauty and fluid light, which had been formed out of the ecstatic union of the

Creative force of God's love and the thoughts of souls wishing only to serve that Divinity—was forever changed. Fear and chaos and suffering and pain—all children parented by judgment and a belief in separation—came to walk the planet with man. Man no longer remembers that he is responsible for creating by his choices the reality in which he finds himself. He has lost touch with the power which that awareness brings— the power to create harmony out of the chaos, strength and soul growth and love out of fear, healing out of suffering and pain.

The source of this great suffering and pain, of all the chaos, is that the actions of humans have been predicated on the erroneous belief that they are separate entities. Yet, there is a driving force at the center of every soul that will not rest until it refutes this belief, surrenders its attachments, lets go of its judgments, and falls gratefully back into the arms of the Creator.

This is where you are today—at the point of surrender. It must be a conscious choice by each soul to offer up once again its will in loving service to the whole, to let go of fear, to forgive those whom you judge harshly, to forgive yourself. By not forgiving, you are rejecting one of your brothers, refusing that soul the opportunity to be healed in love. By not forgiving, you are also closing a part of yourself to the transformative power of God's Love. That Love thrives in openness and expansion. It cannot penetrate a contracted and closed heart. For God respects our choices and will not interfere with our created realities. He will, however, continue to offer us another option, one that is filled with limitless life and love and endless possibilities. One in which the aching longing at the center of every soul is washed away by the overwhelming knowledge that it is never apart from the Creator, who loves unendingly, who makes all things new.

So the form through which you now experience transition— birth and death—is the result of a pattern held in the DNA structure of the human body. It is a reflection of the patterns and collective beliefs of the souls who created this reality. It is not a pattern that was created by God, but one that was established deep in the cellular consciousness of man by choices made by the soul. For out of these choices you have materialized your reality—and at this moment you are in the process of creating it over and over. At any moment you have the freedom to change these basic belief constructs and with them the way that your reality is experienced.

There is coming a time where some of you will transmute your limiting belief structures into the limitless wisdom that there is no true separation between spirit and soul and body, no separation from the whole of creation—only oneness with the Creator. You will surrender your attachments to any particular person, or place, or thing, or experience, or personality construct. There will remain within you only a total embracing of the whole and an awareness in every part of your being of the fluid nature of the universe. Resistance to the fluidity leads only to separation and death.

A surrender to change is what is called for, a release of all resistance to that change in total faith. There is a force at work within your reality, unleashed by the unconscious choices of humans, which will result in the manifestation of many great catastrophes, the loss of many whom you have loved, the loss of structures in which you have placed your faith. These experiences will shake you to your very foundation. They will necessitate a turning inward so that your eyes will be opened to the eternal truth of who you really are. The windows to your consciousness, the door to your hearts will be thrown open to receive God's Grace and His Divine Plan. This perfect pattern will once more come to life in the very cells of your body. Your body will then experience a profound change. It will no longer know separation from the spirit. The bonds that hold you to the darkness of misunderstanding will be dissolved.

In other words, the angels are telling us that if we continue to open our hearts, minds, and souls to the experience of love on a human as well as a Divine level, if we heal all of the imbalances within us that prevent the free flow of this Love through us, then we will undergo a dramatic change at the cellular level. As the result of this change, we will once more experience existence and transition as it was in the beginning.

Great enlightened beings, teachers such as Jesus and White Buffalo Woman, are in possession of such a transformed body. When it was time for them to leave this reality, they did so by raising their vibration to the point that they appeared to those left behind as a great glowing light, which then vanished. Their vibrational frequencies had become too fine to be perceived by the human eye. They merged with the Heaven World without the need to leave any part of themselves behind. They embraced the whole, and so were themselves embraced. This is known as ascension.

The form that your reality has taken has served the whole in that it became a perfect place for you to learn how to take responsibility for what your thought creates and how to appropriately channel energy. Because of the slowed vibrational rate in your world there is a longer time between the thought and the manifestation of that thought. This gives you the opportunity to make alterations in your direction, to rethink things before taking action — to learn to take responsibility for what you have created. At other levels of existence, the time between the thought and the manifestation of that thought is virtually instantaneous. Because the creations of a soul who has not learned to manifest from a will that is at one with Divine will can be devastating — both to the soul and to Creation as a whole — it is most important that this ability is mastered before that soul progresses to these higher frequencies, where unloving thoughts run rampant would have the potential to create unending chaos and destruction.

The thoughts of man energized by the emotions of man have created the reality in which you find yourself. It is the thought of man energized by the emotions of man that will heal and transform this same reality. You and only you have within you the power to do this. The keys to freedom are in the hands of the prisoners. We can offer guidance as to how these keys may be used, but we cannot use them for you. Only you can free yourselves from your self-made prison of contraction and fear.

Some of you will choose to use these keys. You will step out of your prison into the future the Divine intended for you and your world — one filled with love and celebration, with an endless eternal experience of ecstatic creation at many levels of reality. You will return once more to a total awareness of the fluidity of your being and the manifestation of that fluid nature. Your light will shine forth, unimpeded by resistance or contraction. Not one cell in your being will hold the belief that you are separate from love, separate from God. You, and the whole of your reality: the plants, the animals — all that walk or crawl or fly or swim upon the Earth — will be freed to realize the highest potential in an ecstatic dance of light to the harmonies of Creation.

Our Divine teachers are telling us that if we open to Love, the processes of birth and aging and death as we know them will vanish forever and Heaven and Earth will once again merge.

However, there will be others who choose to remain in their self-made dungeon, reluctant to let go of their judgment, their attachment, their belief in separation, their experience of fear. The resulting entrapment in their illusions will create a further slowing of their vibrational frequency, a further dimming of their light. We are fast approaching a time when these two realities — one based on openness and love and unity, the other on contraction and separation and fear — can no longer coexist. At that point you will experience a split in your world. At this time you are not equipped with the mental capacity to understand fully how this will come about; however, the truth of this can be found in your laws of physics. Just know that God loves each soul in his Creation and that this momentous event is necessary so that no soul is held back by another, and so that every soul may receive the experiences it needs to wake up and reclaim its Divine birthright as a conscious co-creator.

We are now in the process of choosing, individually and collectively, how our future will look. What will be the fate of this reality we have created? We are being told that it is up to us. Will we learn through the light of Love and freedom and an acknowledgment of oneness, or through the darkness of separation and pain and suffering? Because these two paths create such divergent vibrational levels, there will be the necessity for the formation of more than one reality in the space that has up to now held a singular experiential arena. This will ensure that we all will receive the lessons we need to grow closer to Great Spirit and to an understanding of who we really are.

The question you need to pose to yourself is this: Do you choose to live your life motivated by love, or by fear? We can empower you with our love, offer encouragement. We can uplift your spirit and hold up your soul, but we cannot make this decision for you. One choice leads to Eternal Life and a complete union of body and spirit to create Heaven on Earth. The other leads only to a continuation of the cycle of birth and death and suffering and pain.

You must learn to focus your energy and come always from the center of your heart where the Truth of Great Spirit speaks loudly. Constantly examine your intent—why you do the things you do, why you make each choice. If in that examination you find that your motivation is anything other than love, then it is wise to delay your action until such time as it becomes an act of love. If this is not possible, then turn away from that action, make another choice; for the result of any action that is not motivated by love is a wound to the heart of the soul, a wound to the heart of God, and a darkening of the light of the world.

Until such time as you have transcended the old patterns that bind you to the wheel of birth and death, you will continue to be subject to this form of entering and leaving your reality. Learn to see death, not as a thing to fear; rather, embrace it as an opportunity to release the part of you that holds any belief that you are separate. See it as an opportunity to regain the pure freedom of spirit to love fully, to give full expression to all that you are, to continue to learn and grow in love and understanding. If you are willing to focus on love rather than fear during this experience of leaving your reality for the next, you will then be open to all the wonder that awaits you on the other side.

Remember that fear does not exist outside of your own consciousness. In fact, you are the creator of this fear. You called it into being to serve as a protector from that which you believe to be a painful and potentially annihilating experience, a change to be avoided and resisted at all costs. This fear, and the contraction that accompanies its manifestation, rather than protecting you from pain, becomes the very source of that deep suffering. Because you have created this fear, only you have the power to transmute the emotional energy trapped in this form that is not serving you. You can speak to your fear, thank it for its attempt to serve you. Then, by transferring your faith in that fear's protective power to a surrender to God's Love in faith, you will unequivocally be supported and comforted and guided gently to a place that holds the healing and love your soul craves.

Stay focused on this Great Love that is a part of all that is. Center your awareness on the unending and immutable connection with everything that ever is or was or will be, and the transition known as death will not be made in fear and despair, but consciously, openly, with joyous expectation. This event of transcendent beauty will then be experienced for what it truly is—a release of the greatest, most magnificent part of us to fly free of the darkness, out of the shadows that blind us so that we may once again greet God face to face. At that moment we will finally see the mystery of who we are reflected back to us in the blindingly bright visage of the Divine. We will truly be at peace with the Creator, at peace in our hearts. We will in the end be Home.

Also by Richard Preston
First Light
American Steel
The Hot Zone
The Cobra Event
The Demon in the Freezer

The Boat
of Dreams
A CHRISTMAS STORY

Richard Preston

Illustrations by
George Henry Jennings

A TOUCHSTONE BOOK
Published by Simon & Schuster
NEW YORK LONDON TORONTO SYDNEY SINGAPORE

TOUCHSTONE
Rockefeller Center
1230 Avenue of the Americas
New York, NY 10020

For information regarding special discounts for bulk purchases,
please contact Simon & Schuster Special Sales at
1-800-456-6798 or business@simonandschuster.com

Designed by Joy O'Meara Battista

Manufactured in the United States of America

1   3   5   7   9   10   8   6   4   2

Library of Congress Cataloging-in-Publication Data
Preston, Richard.
The boat of dreams : a Christmas story / Richard Preston.
p.   cm.
"A Touchstone book."
I. Title.
PS3566.R4126B63 2003   813'54—dc21   2003054417

ISBN 0-7432-4592-X

In memory of a friend
Robin Bloksberg
I wanted to tell you a story . . .

The author is dedicating a portion of his proceeds

from this book to medical research in the

Women's Cancer Program at the Dana-Farber Cancer Institute.

I wrote this book originally for just one person. She was a lifelong friend who was dying of breast cancer, leaving a husband and a five-year-old daughter. I had nothing to give them except a story. A story is only words, but sometimes a story is the best we have to give. *The Boat of Dreams* was written as a gift, and so it can be passed along in the same spirit.

The Boat of Dreams

A CHRISTMAS STORY

Part One
THE CHRISTMAS GHOST

the hauntings in our trailer began before Christmas, 1969, in the months after we learned that Dad had died in a rice paddy in Vietnam. In those days we were living in our old Glidemaster. It was a single-wide trailer with tail fins and a broken taillight and plenty of dents. Dad had called it the Crashmaster. He had bought it for a hundred dollars from a man in Rockland, and he towed it down the coast of Maine to New Harbor, where he had found for rent a meadow overlooking the sea. I should say that we were my father, William T. Foster Sr., and my mother, Sarah Ann, and my little sister, Lila, and me—Will T. Foster Jr.

My father was a lobster fisherman. He had two hundred and fifty lobster traps. His traps were made of bent pieces of oak. He set his traps on the bottom of the ocean, attached to brightly colored buoys. He went smelled of the sea, but at that moment he smelled of balsam fir—he smelled of Christmas.

"Santa Claus," he said to my sister, "has got more tricks up his sleeve than you could ever imagine. You would be amazed at all the ways he has of getting into a trailer. But we'd better leave the door unlocked. Santa can get pretty desperate with trailers, and we don't want him using his wrecking bar."

"Daddy!" Lila clapped her hand over her mouth.

Mom got a little annoyed with Dad for telling Lila about Santa's wrecking bar. "It's made of peppermint candy, Lila, and it won't affect a Glidemaster," she explained.

Lila wasn't so sure. She wrote a sign with a crayon, and Dad helped her tape it to the door:

He got the message. We awoke on Christmas morning with presents heaped on the feet of our bunks. Lila had the bottom bunk and I had the top bunk. We sat up in our sleeping bags and tore open our presents. I couldn't believe my eyes: I got a baseball with Jim Lonborg's actual real autograph on it. Jim Lonborg was a pitcher for the Boston Red Sox. Santa gave Lila a stuffed white baby seal.

"He's Chicken Bones!" Lila yelled, after she opened her present.

We started laughing. "Why did you name him that?" Mom asked.

"Don't ask me why," Lila said with a shrug.

Mom cooked a turkey in the little electric oven. It got burned and smoked a little, and she started crying. Then she could not stop crying. Dad was in the Army Reserves, and a notice had come before Christmas that he was being called overseas. We held hands around the dinette table and sang Christmas carols. "This is the best Christmas *ever,*" Lila declared, clutching Chicken Bones Don't-Ask-Me-Why.

Two weeks later it was time for Dad to go for his call-up. I was out by the gear shed with him, helping him put everything away before he left. He was sorting through all his tools, and he said, "You don't need to worry about me, Bud, I'm too old for combat. They're putting me in a maintenance crew with the older guys. I can fix anything."

He was thirty-three. I followed him out through the door of the shed, and he stood before all his lobstering gear, surveying it with satisfaction, his hands on his hips. The *Sarah Ann* rested in her winter cradle beside a small spruce tree. His two hundred and fifty traps were piled in a giant stack near the boat, neat, square, and perfect. He had put up large coils of the stiff rope we call buoy warp, and he had piled up all his lobster buoys in a mountain of white and blue. Those were my father's buoy colors, white and blue, and they always reminded me of clouds in the summer sky.

"Everything is shipshape," my father said. Suddenly he yelled, "Barber scratch!" and he grabbed me and started rubbing my head with his knuckles, scruffing up my hair. I pretended I was trying to escape, but I could not let go of my father at that moment. He stopped giving me a barber scratch and put his arm around me and said, "When I get back, I think you'll be big enough to be my stern man once in a while."

And then we walked across the meadow back to the trailer, just me and my dad. He had his arm around me, and we didn't say anything. The next day he was gone.

A government car came slowly up our dirt driveway past the stone wall and the white pine trees, and stopped. An army captain knocked on the door. He held his stiff pressed cap in his hands, and he would not sit down. He informed us that Dad had been killed in action near Phu Loc. We had never heard of Phu Loc. He had been shot in the chest, the captain explained, and they had tried to carry him out of the rice paddy, but they had been in combat and under heavy fire, and he had slipped out of their hands into the water and had been lost. The captain handed Dad's dog tags to Mom. His hand was trembling. He explained that he had been one of the men carrying Dad. Dad's tags had torn off in his hands.

"Where's Daddy?" Lila asked. She looked at Mom.

Very gently, Mom took Lila to her, and her hand found mine. For a time it seemed that she could not speak. "Was there . . . anything . . . left . . . of my husband?"

The captain didn't answer for a while. "He asked me to say something to you, ma'am."

Her tears were running. "What?"

"To say he loved you."

Mom whispered: "Oh, Will . . . Will . . . Will . . ."

She kept saying his name, as if she were calling for him across the infinite emptiness of time and space and of his not being with us now or forever again. I remember her face so shining with tears that her grief seemed to fill our trailer with light.

I was thirteen, too old to let people see me cry. I did my crying at night in the top bunk, inside my sleeping bag. I sobbed into my pillow, and I tore the flannel of the sleeping bag with my teeth, but there was nothing I could do to make the world go a different way. My father had died an unknown soldier.

We were short of money, and Mom knew she had to sell Dad's boat and his lobstering gear in order to make ends meet. She had taken a job as a cashier at the supermarket in Damariscotta when he went away, but it didn't pay very well. The *Sarah Ann* sat in its cradle in the meadow near the little spruce tree, not far from the heap of buoys and the stack of traps. Her white paint had started to weather and turn gray, and her foredeck was covered with an old piece of canvas that slatted in the wind.

The boat was beautiful. She had been built in Friendship by the Swett brothers in 1942, and her original name had been the *Dora*. Edgar Swett and his brother, Art, were famous for their wooden boats. Art Swett was blind, but he could fair a plank with a sense of touch, and he could cut perfect structures in wood with a small chisel. Some people thought Art was speechless as well as blind. Art Swett knew very well how to talk, but he considered it a waste of time, life being short and the work of building wooden boats being long. The only person he ever spoke with was his brother, and they say the longest thing he ever said to him was, "I have mislaid the small chisel, Edgar, and I cannot find it."

The *Dora* was the last boat the Swett brothers made before they closed their shop and retired. They used up their best stock on that boat. It was stock they had been keeping around their yard for years, saving it for the right boat, but the right boat never quite came along, so in the end they used it all on a lobster boat. They used their finest knees, cut from the roots of giant hackmatack trees that had grown for long ages in Aroostook swamps. They used their best crooks made of black locust, and they used massive chunks of Connecticut white oak, and they used wide beautiful clear flitches of cedar planking that were far too fine for use in any regular boat. They gave her a tall, brave stem, and her sheer was sprung with confidence. Her wheel house was raked to an angle of perfection, and her cuddy cabin had those old-fashioned diamond-paned windows that are so pretty. Her gunwales tapered to a narrow, gentle stern, with a cambered stern deck and the right amount of tumblehome. When the Swett brothers bent the cedar planks to the oak frames of that hull, I believe they had given up on the world and were trying to please only the eye of God.

Mom and Dad were married at nineteen, when he

was in the army. After his discharge, he crewed on a fishing boat, and he serviced Sears washing machines for a while, but he always dreamed of owning his own lobster boat. He was forever running off to look at some old lobster boat that was for sale somewhere. The problem was that he could not afford a good one.

At last he came across the *Dora,* sitting in a yard in Pemaquid. She had ended up with a lobster fisherman named Harold Poland. He had run her hard and had not kept her up, but the sea had not hated this boat. Dad paid Harold's price without argument and renamed her the *Sarah Ann.* Then, naturally, the boat needed a lot of fixing up. That's why we were living in that trailer. With the way Dad was pouring money into his lobster boat, we could not afford a double-wide.

After he had spent his last dime repairing the hull, he had no money left to spend on a new engine. So he had to use the engine that Harold had put in her. It was an automobile engine from a Studebaker Lark. That Studebaker engine in the *Sarah Ann* was anything but a lark. It whined and chattered, burned oil like an outboard motor, and laid a cloud of blue smoke. Not only that, the boat's steering wheel was an automobile steering wheel—from a Studebaker Lark. Apparently Harold Poland had enjoyed the sensation of lobstering with a Lark.

The waters of Muscongus Bay are treacherous. The bay is a maze of drowned ledges and breakers, where surf rolls continually over rocks just under the surface. If your engine dies near a ledge or a breaker, your boat can be swept onto the rocks. If your boat sinks and you end up in the water, and the water is very cold, as it is in spring or fall in Maine, you may have only minutes before you lose consciousness and drown. Quite a few lobster fishermen do not know how to swim; they feel there is no point in knowing. When Dad was pulling traps out by the Devil's Elbow, you could hear his engine all the way past Wreck Island, giving off a yammering sound that said, *Failure is not an option—let's hope.*

Dad was forever tinkering with the *Sarah Ann* when it was up in its cradle in our meadow. We'd hear *kerklunk, kerklunk* as he worked the clutch, and then, "Aw—*what* is wrong now?" Meanwhile he listened to the Red Sox on the boat's radio. During the Impossible Dream of 1967, when the Red Sox almost won the

World Series, but didn't, we heard words coming out of that boat that could have made its caulk fall out. (The dream was impossible, of course, since we are talking about the Red Sox.) He also listened to the top-forty hits and he'd start singing with Tommy James & the Shondells:

"I think we're alone now
The beating of our hearts is the only sou-und . . ."

And when the song got to

"'Cause what would they SAYYYYYYYYY . . ."

his voice went all high and screechy until he sounded like an electric saw eating into plywood.

"Cut it out, Will! That's driving me crazy," Mom would yell from the window of the trailer.

"It's our song! Sing it with me."

"Stop it!"

But then she would start singing. Mom's voice was beautiful; you could hear it all over the meadow. Pretty soon they would have a duet going between the trailer and the boat. Sometimes it would end with their going off and shutting themselves in the bedroom at the end of the trailer.

"What are they doing in there?" Lila said to me one day. She was sitting on the rug by the recliner chair, sucking her thumb.

I just rolled my eyes.

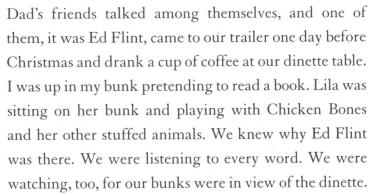

Dad's friends talked among themselves, and one of them, it was Ed Flint, came to our trailer one day before Christmas and drank a cup of coffee at our dinette table. I was up in my bunk pretending to read a book. Lila was sitting on her bunk and playing with Chicken Bones and her other stuffed animals. We knew why Ed Flint was there. We were listening to every word. We were watching, too, for our bunks were in view of the dinette.

Ed Flint was a short, bony man with dark eyebrows, and he did not look at people directly. For that reason some people called him Shifty Ed. He had a reputation

Suddenly Lila was tugging at me. Her eyes were wide. "Willie? There's somebody in the bathroom."

I scrambled down from my bunk, and we stood in the little hallway. There was a thumping sound coming from inside the bathroom of our trailer.

I walked closer to the bathroom door and listened. Then I heard a raspy voice inside the bathroom, saying something like, ". . . stupid tub . . ."

"Who's that?" I said loudly.

No answer. I put my hand on the doorknob. My heart was pounding.

"Willieee, it's a ghost!" Lila squealed.

I opened the door.

It was a tiny bathroom, with a sink and a mirror, a toilet, a small bathtub that had a shower hose, and a frosted window.

The bathroom was steamy, and there was a smell of sweat in it. The mirror had fogged up, and there was a dab of shaving cream on it; and there was a handprint on the glass.

Dad smelled like sweat when he had been working on the boat, and he had always wiped the mirror with his hand when he shaved. These recollections filled my chest with a rush of terrible loneliness mixed with a quiver of hope.

"Dad?"

A chill seemed to swirl in the air. The handprint on the mirror was an absence, not a hand but a hole in the shape of a hand, like a piece missing from a jigsaw puzzle. If his spirit had touched the mirror, he had gone far away now, and I could feel it.

I shut the door.

"Was it a ghost?" my sister asked.

"It was nothing."

The idea that the unknown visitor in our trailer might have been Dad both excited and terrified me. We did not have a clear picture of what had happened to him in the rice paddy at Phu Loc. All the army captain would say was that he "had been unable to hold his head above the water after taking bullets in the chest." The thought of my father dying that way was almost unbearable for me. What if he came to us covered with mud and blood? From what I knew of ghosts, they often came in the form they had last had on earth.

At the same time, I had to consider the possibility that the haunting might not be Dad. This was a used trailer. Someone could have died in it. Maybe that was why the man in Rockland had sold it to Dad for just a hundred dollars—he had wanted to get rid of it.

The next day, the school bus let us off at the end of the driveway. I was nervous about going home. I told myself that maybe the visitation had been a freak. Maybe it wouldn't happen again. We walked up the driveway, and when we got to the top, we saw an unfamiliar car parked next to the trailer. A stranger was sitting in the car.

The door opened, and he got out. He was a round man in a puffy down jacket. His hair was combed over a bald spot, and he was wearing pressed trousers and shiny shoes. When he got out of the car, his trousers started flapping in the wind coming off the sea. The wind got under his hair and flipped it up straight off his bald patch. "Where's your mother?"

"This is private property. Who are you?"

"I know it's private property. I own it."

His name was Bob Thacker. Dad had rented the meadow from him, but we had never met him before. He was a real-estate man who lived much of the time in Florida.

Mr. Thacker kept his hands in his jacket and turned around slowly, looking at everything—at the Glidemaster, the metal shed, the heap of lobster buoys, the stack of traps, the *Sarah Ann*. "I've got some people who might want to buy this lot. They're going to be here right after Christmas. This old boat needs to be taken out of here. It ruins the view." He glanced at me. "Where's your mother?"

"She's working."

"What did you say?" The wind was strong.

"She's working."

"Where?"

"The supermarket."

"What supermarket?"

"The one in Damariscotta."

"What time does she get off?"

"Five."

He looked at his watch and peered through the gloom toward our unlit trailer. "So she's left her kids alone in the town dump." He got back into his car. "I'm coming back later. You tell your mother to have her checkbook ready. She owes me a lot of rent." There was a roar, and his car bounced down our driveway, its taillights glowing.

Inside the trailer, it was as cold as a deep freeze. I switched on the oil burner, but it never seemed to get the trailer warm enough. The wind was hissing in the windows, and we could hear the New Harbor bell buoy going *clong, clong.*

"We're leaving," I said to Lila.

"Where are we going, Willie?"

"Don't call me Willie. My name is Will."

Lila grabbed Chicken Bones from her bunk, and we cut down the hill toward Back Cove and passed along a wooden footbridge that crosses over the water of the cove, Lila clutching Chicken Bones and hurrying after me, her feet going *thumpity thump* on the boards. "Wait! Wait for me and Chicken Bones!"

Along the edges of Back Cove there are piers with work sheds on top of them. There are always men working around the sheds and piers, for some of them fish all winter. I led my sister to the tide line beneath the sheds, because you could always find interesting things washed up among the piers.

Just then we heard voices. We were standing among some pilings directly underneath a shed on a pier. Up above our heads, we could see floorboards and lines of light shining through cracks.

". . . the most stubborn woman." It was Ed Flint speaking.

"I can't stand going up there anymore. That crazy old trailer and those dirty-looking kids." It was Brian Hanscom.

"That's a Swett boat," another voice said.

"Nice boat."

"Nice for firewood," Ed Flint said.

"You liar, Ed. You covet that boat."

"I made her an offer."

There was laughter. Someone said, "What, for fifty cents?"

"It was fair," Flint said stubbornly.

"Will did a decent job fixing it up," someone said.

"That engine is no good."

"Bennett Chase made Sarah an offer for the boat, did you hear that?"

"No!"

"Yes. She refused it," Brian Hanscom said. "That little girl is a holy terror. She cursed me out."

"I did n—" Lila began.

"Shh!" I put my hand over her mouth.

"Thacker is kicking them off. He's getting them evicted."

"Evicted? Who told you that?"

"Thacker."

"Well, he owns the land." It was Brian Hanscom's voice.

"Aren't there any relatives in the picture?"

"Nope. Will and Sarah were kind of alone in the world."

"Those kids are going to end up in the state home. Or they'll end up homeless."

Lila was standing there, holding Chicken Bones against her stomach, and I was gripping her. She started shivering uncontrollably. "I'm cold."

"Be quiet," I said to her in a low voice. But my heart was pounding like a hammer. The state home? Evicted? Homeless? Didn't Mr. Thacker know about how Dad had given his life for our country?

I took my sister by the hand and pulled her up the hill toward the village.

"Where are we going, Willie?"

"Just be quiet."

I had no idea where we were going. The road went alongside the harbor, climbing the hill. New Harbor was a narrow inlet that opened on the sea. It looked as if something had taken a huge ax and split the land in that place. Inside the split, ghostly white lobster boats and seine-fishing boats rested at their moorings, floating in water as black as oil. Here and there on the piers a brilliant work light glowed like a star, throwing a splash of illumination over the shapes of men working, and we heard the whine of a pump going somewhere. Rising up the hillsides above the piers stood the houses of New Harbor. Their windows glowed with electric candles for the Christmas season, and a bare lilac bush by one house was strung with colored lights. The front doors held wreaths made of balsam or white pine, and tendrils of smoke mixed with a soft sweetness hung in the air, for someone was burning logs of sugar maple. It was Christmas in Maine, with all that meant to me. My heart ached for Christmas, yet I did not want it to come, for I knew that this Christmas would bring only memories we could not bear.

We passed a big square house that had a porch facing the sea.

"Let's go see Lola and Courtland," my sister said.

Courtland Brackett was a retired captain of a seine-fishing boat. Dad had crewed with him, and that was when Dad got the dimple on his chin, when he was hit with a winch. Dad had learned about the sea from Courtland Brackett. "Never trust the sea. She is mean," Courtland had said to my father.

Lila ran up the Bracketts' driveway and knocked on the back door.

A light went on, and Lola Brackett opened the door. She was a small lady with tightly curled hair that she wore underneath a hair net. She had spectacles and bright eyes.

"Well! Come in! You look like you need a sinker."

A sinker is a doughnut cooked in lard.

We sat in the Bracketts' parlor, rubbing ourselves to warm up.

Lola went into the kitchen and came out with a plate of sinkers.

Meanwhile, Courtland Brackett was sitting on the couch. He had a round, ruddy face, and he was nearly bald, with a fringe of white hair and sharp blue eyes, and an interesting grin.

We started eating the sinkers. You could not hardly breathe with a sinker in your mouth. You had to kind of breathe around it. It gave you the hiccups, so Lola brought us glasses of milk to cure them. When the cold milk hit the lard, the lard froze and stuck to the roof of your mouth in a layer of solid fat. Then you had to run your tongue over the fat to melt it. This kept us busy for a while.

"A sinker," Courtland said, "will stick to your chest and nourish you all day."

"Cuh I huv anuh . . . hic?" my sister asked.

"Why, help yourself," Lola said.

The sinkers were definitely sticking to our chests.

✳

No sinker can last forever. Hiccuping and chocked with

sinkers. The Bracketts were not home, and we ended up back at the trailer.

I got the key from my pocket and opened the door. A smell of sweat hung in the air.

A shape was sitting in the recliner chair in front of the television set. The television was on and glowing blue in the dark, and the show was *The Edge of Night*. The shape was just a little wavery, like water rippling in a tide pool, which made me suspect it was a ghost. The shape's back was to us, and we could not see its face. For a moment my heart leaped into my throat—maybe it was Dad!

I turned on the light.

We saw a thick, seamed, old, weather-beaten neck. We saw the back of a blocklike head with a stiff, gray, whiffle crew cut—not at all like Dad's brown hair. We could see the ghost's scalp shining through his crew cut, the way it does with older men. He was wearing a wool shirt and green work pants, suspenders, and boots. It was pretty obviously the ghost of a lobster fisherman, but it was not Dad. I felt a wave of disappointment.

"Urrrp"—we heard a belch. The ghost's hand came

lard, we trudged back to the trailer in the dark and when we got there, Mr. Thacker's car was parked next to Mom's car. We found him and Mom sitting at the kitchenette table, with folders full of papers between them.

"You are seven months behind in the rent, Mrs. Foster. If you don't pay it, you will be evicted."

"I'm looking for a better job. We lost our fishing income when my husband was called to the service—"

"I do know what happened. I am sorry, of course."

He didn't sound sorry.

Lila squinted at me. "Hic," she said. She still had the sinker hiccups.

I glared at her: don't say anything.

"My husband died for our country."

"I am sorry, but that's not the point. This is a valuable property with a bold ocean view. It is not meant for people in trailers."

"I have nowhere to go with my children."

He pursed his lips together. "There are all sorts of trailer parks down south of here." He turned his head and looked out the window at the *Sarah Ann*. "I want this lobster boat removed immediately. It is an eyesore. I have some people coming to look at the property the day after Christmas, and that old boat makes my property look like . . . a junkyard. You could sell the boat and pay the rent you owe me. I'm trying to help you."

She stood up and backed away from the dinette. "Get yourself off."

Calmly he gathered his papers and stood up. "All right . . . I'll sell the boat."

"What do you mean?"

"You don't own it, Mrs. Foster."

"It's all I do own."

"Your husband had no money when he bought it. He borrowed the money from me."

"That's a lie," my mother said desperately.

Mr. Thacker opened a folder. He put on a pair of reading glasses and sorted through it. He shook out a paper and put his finger on it. "There's his signature. William T. Foster. On a promissory note for four thousand dollars."

"The boat's not worth that!"

"It's what he paid for it. Rather, what I paid for it."

"Oh, Will . . . oh, Will."

"He came to me for a business loan. He said the lobstering business had never been better."

My sister sat down on her bunk. She was staring at Mr. Thacker. "Hic."

He opened the door and picked his way down our cinderblock steps. He looked up at us through the door. "Your children are living in squalor. I have reported the situation to the authorities. These children may have to be removed for their own good."

Just then the wind got under his hair flap and flipped it up straight, and his hair started waving around his bald patch.

My sister hopped up from her bunk and ran to the door and screeched after him, "Merry Christmas, Mr. Dumwad! I hope you burst a blood vessel in your head! Hic!"

His car door slammed.

🌿

The next day, when the school bus let us off at our driveway, I took Lila to the Bracketts' house to get some

into view, holding a can of beer. The hand placed the can on the rug. It was a huge, massive hand, gnarly with veins and tendons.

"What are you doing here?" my sister asked.

"Quiet, I'm trying to watch this show." The ghost had a raspy voice.

"Don't talk to it," I whispered to my sister. "It'll leave in a minute."

"Are you a ghost?" Lila said in a clear voice.

"What do you think?" It turned around in the chair and looked at us.

When I saw that face, I thought I would die. The face was not evil, but it was terrifying, and the ghost had the deepest eyes. It was definitely a specter, for when he turned to look at us, I could see *The Edge of Night* glowing through his head. I was so scared I almost puked.

My sister was unfazed. "Are you somebody that died?"

The ghost snorted. "Huh. Is the Pope Catholic?"

"How come you're drinking beer?" Lila asked.

"It's not beer, it's ale," the ghost answered. "Now let me watch this show."

My sister was not to be stopped. "Why are you here?"

"There is a need in this place," the ghost's voice came softly over his shoulder. "There is a need for your dreams."

"What dreams?" Lila demanded.

"Shut *up*," I whispered to her.

The ghost turned around again in the chair, and his stare chilled me to my bones. There was something about that face that seemed familiar. "Don't say shut up to your sister."

Lila pulled Chicken Bones tight against her stomach and said in a small voice, "How did you die, Mr. Ghost?"

Just then, we heard the sound of Mom's car coming up the driveway, and he vanished. There was a rippling feeling in the air, like the passing of a wake through the world itself, and the ghost was gone.

"Mommy! We saw a ghost! He had wicked B.O.! He told Willie not to say shut up!" Lila said excitedly.

Mom looked at me. "Was there somebody in here?"

"No," I said truthfully, since it wasn't somebody, it was a ghost. I didn't want her to think our trailer was haunted. She didn't need that.

Mom put a bag of groceries on the dinette table and pulled a strand of hair off her face. She took Lila in her arms. "We all sometimes feel there are ghosts, Lila."

The weather reports told of a blizzard coming, so I went out beyond the stone wall and cut our Christmas tree. It was a small red spruce. I set it up in the living area, where it filled our trailer with an agreeable scent of the woods. The next day, when we got off the school bus, the sky was flat gray, and tiny glittery snowflakes, like powdered glass, had begun to sift through the air, a sign of a winter storm beginning to break. We hurried up to Reilly's Market and got snacks, but we didn't stop off at the Bracketts' house for sinkers because we wanted to get home before the storm hit. As we crossed the footbridge over Back Cove, Lila was full of talk about the ghost. "I think he's kind of nice," she said.

"No way. He's a mean one."

"He's just grumpy, Willie."

"The grumpy ones can go psycho on you in a hurry."

"He's not a screamer, anyway," she said.

"He'll be screaming right fast if you keep talking back at him. That's a risky thing to do with a ghost."

She stopped on the bridge and put her finger in her mouth and touched a tooth. "I have a wiggler, Willie."

"Call me Willie again, and you'll have a whole bunch of wigglers."

She probed her loose tooth with her finger.

"You keep doing that, and you'll be bleeding all over the place. Just don't come to me for sympathy."

"I wonder what's his name."

"What, the ghost?"

"Yeah."

"I dunno. Somebody died in our trailer, is my guess."

"I can get my tongue under it."

"Cut it out, this is serious."

We started walking up the hill. Lila was still working her tooth with her finger.

"Don't say anything to Mom—"

There were lights flashing in our driveway. Lights flashing in a haze of snow coming down.

There was a truck parked in our driveway. It was

towing a flatbed trailer. And there was a police car with its bubble lights going blue-white, blue-white, blue-white. The police officer was from Bremen—Mr. Thacker had brought him—and the officer was standing next to Mom and talking to her. Mr. Thacker was standing off to one side with his hands in his down jacket and his hair up in a flap. They had set pipes for rollers, and they were getting ready to winch the cradle and the boat onto the flatbed trailer. Mr. Thacker was taking possession of Dad's boat.

Mom stood there as still as ice. Lila and I ran up to her, and Lila grabbed Mom and clung to her. I stood there not knowing what to do. Lila started crying. Mom pulled off Lila's hood and smoothed her hair and put her hood back on, then told her not to worry, Sweetie, it's only a boat.

"But it's Daddy's boat!" Lila wailed.

They had just dragged the *Sarah Ann* onto the trailer when the storm hit in full force. The men's shouts were lost in the wind, yet Mom continued to stand there. She refused to go indoors, but she told us to go inside. The wind began to cry in the windows, and the white pines were sighing. Pretty soon the snow was driving sideways and sweeping into the black sea, and the surf was crashing. They backed the truck around to try to get it pointed down the driveway. I kept looking out the window. Mom was standing in front of the truck, blocking it.

"Please stand aside, Mrs. Foster!" one of the men yelled.

"Put down my husband's boat!" she yelled back at them.

I ran outdoors. "Come inside, Mom, please!"

She wouldn't get out of the way.

"Move her," Mr. Thacker said.

But the police officer would not move her. None of the men would touch her, either. They all seemed a little afraid of her. The storm was filling the driveway rapidly with snow. They had to abandon the truck and the flatbed trailer with the boat sitting on it.

They put a chain over the *Sarah Ann,* running it across her gunwales and down to the trailer, and they padlocked the chain so that nobody could move the boat. Mr. Thacker drove off with the key to the padlock. He barely got out of our driveway. His car skidded all the way down it.

Mom continued to stand in the driveway, and the storm became terrible.

"You're going to freeze, Mom!" I said to her. I was almost crying.

"I'll be in in a little while." She just kept standing in the storm with her eyes on Dad's boat, as if she could not let it out of her sight for fear it would disappear. She turned as white as a statue. I went back to the trailer and got Lila ready for bed. Finally, Mom came indoors. She was rimed with snow and shaking with cold, but she got her coat off and helped us say our prayers. The wind was just slamming at the metal walls of the trailer.

"This may be the first time a lobster boat was ever saved by a Northeaster," she said to us with a little smile, shaking with cold.

I was glad to see her smile. But the boat wasn't saved. Sooner or later they would come back for the *Sarah Ann*. No storm can last forever.

The next morning the storm was still blowing. Mom didn't call anyone to plow us out. Even so, she had to go to work at the supermarket. She had parked her car down by the road. I walked down the driveway with her and helped her shovel it out.

"If anybody comes, call the store manager and have him get me. You can make hot cocoa." She drove off into the whirling snow.

Lila and I decorated the tree with a few ornaments. It wasn't the same as Dad's beautiful tree the year before, but at least we had one. The storm became fitful, so we went outdoors to play. I helped Lila make snow angels, sweeping her arms and legs in the snow. I climbed up on the truck and examined the chain around Dad's boat. The ocean was wild and plastered with reaching combers. It was time for some cocoa, so we headed back for the trailer.

I opened the door, and a wave of B.O. slapped us like a sour dishrag. The TV was blaring, and we heard snoring. The ghost had fallen asleep lying on his back in the recliner, and his stomach poked up in a huge mound. That heaped-up stomach of his looked like the burial site of ten thousand sinkers cooked in lard.

The mound stirred. "Make yourselves at home."

"You did, anyway," I said. Those were the first words I had spoken to the ghost.

Lila opened the door of the bathroom . . . and slammed it. "Ew! He did a stinky one in there."

The ghost's scalp turned red—you could see it flaming through his crew cut—and he muttered something about how there's no such thing as privacy in a single-wide.

Lila plumped herself down on her bunk. "Guess what, Mr. Ghost, we're gonna have a white Christmas."

"Those are my favorite kind," the ghost rumbled.

"Me, too," Lila said. "I just love snowstorms, 'specially in a trailer. Don't you, Mr. Ghost?"

"Trailers make me cranky."

"I think they make you stinky. I'm Lila." She held up her baby seal. "This is Chicken Bones Don't-Ask-Me-Why."

The ghost turned around in the chair. There was a serious look on his red, weather-beaten face. "Why shouldn't I ask you why?"

"Because it's just his name, that's why."

"Oh."

"What's your name Mr. Ghost?"

"Well—you can call me Dexter, little girl."

"I'm not a little girl. I'm seven."

The ghost pulled the lever on the recliner, and slowly he brought himself upright, giving my sister a narrow look. "Well, young lady, I see you have a few opinions, don't you?"

"Yeah. You need a bath."

He looked startled. "Well, I tried to take a bath! But I don't fit in your bathtub. It's one of those cheesy little plastic tubs they put in trailers. I hate trailers. They give me problems."

"It's because you're too fat," Lila said.

"I am not fat! I am merely stout."

"He's not just fat, he's an idiot," I said out of the corner of my mouth to Lila. "He doesn't even know how to use a shower hose."

Our visitor glared at me, then started trying to get himself up from the chair. He struggled and lurched, but he couldn't stand up.

"Ha-ha, you're stuck in the chair." Lila giggled.

Suddenly Dexter jerked to his feet. The back of the recliner snapped forward with a thud. "That chair is no good."

"Not after you sat in it," Lila shot back.

"I think we're ticking him off," I whispered to her.

Dexter edged himself around our Christmas tree. It looked as if he was headed for the bathroom. The floor shook as he moved, making the glass balls on our Christmas tree sparkle and bounce around on the boughs. I thought he was a fairly heavy one for a ghost.

He went into the little bathroom, and the door clicked shut. My sister and I looked at each other. Who ever heard of a ghost taking a shower? There was a hiss as the shower came on. Steam started coming from under the door.

Our supernatural visitor must have been in a Christmasy kind of mood, because his voice suddenly rang out, all hoarse and cracked:

> *"Angels we have heard on high*
> *Sweetly singing o'er the plains,*
> *And the mountains in reply*
> *Echoing their joyous strains!"*

Then he went into the "gloria" part:

"Glo orrr, oh-oh-oh-oh orr, oh-oh . . . uck! Hawk! Huwughkkkk!"

He hucked up a looey and spat it in the shower—*thwap*. "Gotta try something easier," he muttered. He broke into

"Si-i-ilent night . . . holyy-y-y-y-y . . . CRIKEY!"

There was a tremendous BOOM! Our trailer shook so hard it almost tipped off its cinderblocks.

Silence.

We listened. Waited.

Lila squinted at me. "What happened, Willie?"

"Hopefully he exploded."

Silence.

"I'm scared, Willie."

"He probably just went into another dimension," I said.

"What if he died?"

"He already did that." I thumped on the wall with my hand. "Yo, Dexter! Are you all right in there?"

Silence. I tried the door. It wouldn't open.

"It's locked, Willie!"

"I *know* it's locked. Don't worry, he probably just took a heart attack."

"Do they take heart attacks?"

"I have no idea." I rattled the door. "Hey Dexter—open up."

"Willie?"

"What? And quit calling me Willie."

"Does ghosts have brains?"

"What are you talking about?"

"He could of burst a blood vessel in his head."

"So what do you want me to do, call an ambulance?"

"Yes!" she said.

"Forget it."

"Please?"

"No way."

"You have to!"

"An ambulance isn't going to solve this ghost's problems, believe me."

"But he's hurt, Willie!"

A disturbing thought was beginning to trouble me: What if our visitor was *not* a ghost? What if he was some crazy old man who had been breaking into our trailer and playing some kind of joke on us? If a dead man turned up in our bathtub, there would be trouble.

Finally, I went to the telephone and dialed the operator. "Can you get me Miles Memorial Hospital? Thank you. Hello? Yes, this is William T. Foster Jr., down to New Harbor. There's an old guy here who got sick in our trailer. He's locked in the bathroom. We can't get a sound out of him—"

"He burst a blood vessel in his head!" my sister screamed over my shoulder.

"Can you bring a wrecking bar? We need to get him out of there."

Just then we heard: "Owwww . . . I think I broke my coccyx."

"Never mind. False alarm." I hung up.

Lila squinted at me. "*What* did he break?"

"His tailbone."

Lila started giggling. "Dexter took a butt attack!"

"*Who said that?!*" Dexter roared at us through the wall. Then he started banging around, struggling to stand up. "It's not funny when you break your tailbone," he rumbled, "and do you know why? It's because you can't wear a cast on your rear end, that's why. The bones don't heal straight, and you end up with a crooked fanny." He heard us laughing. "It's not funny!" He went on to remark that a spirit these days needs to have an accident lawyer on a retainer just to be able to visit a blankety-blank trailer.

Finally he came out of our bathroom, wrapped modestly in a towel, with his clothes draped over his arm and his stomach leading the way. "What are you two staring at?" he said, throwing us a look that would slay. He was headed for Mom's bedroom.

"Don't go in there," I said to the ghost.

"I need somewhere to dress." The door clicked shut.

"I told you to stay out of there!"

No reply. The trailer creaked, and we heard his suspenders snap as he pulled them over his shoulders. Finally he came out.

I stood in front of him and crossed my arms. "Who are you, anyway? Your name isn't Dexter."

"Stand aside, boy."

"You're such a liar."

He lost it. He started yelling at me in a booming voice: "I never lie, boy! Never! Don't ever call me a liar!"

"Try not to get tense," I said. "It'll make your sweat problem worse."

"Do you have any idea who I really am? Do you have any idea what I could do to you? You have *no* idea, boy." The ghost shouldered past me and plumped down in the recliner and wouldn't look at us.

"Did anybody ever tell you what a stupid name Dexter is?"

There was a growl. "It's my middle name." He kept his back turned to me.

"Is the rest of it just as stupid?" I said.

"It happens to be Dexter Claws."

I burst out laughing. "The ghost is mental! He thinks he's a lobster."

"My first name—one of them—is Nicholas. The last name is spelled C-L-A-U-S."

There was a moment of dead silence.

Lila and I looked at each other.

Nicholas D. Claus.

We looked back at our ghost. He was keeping his face turned away from us.

Our visitor was rather roly-poly. His large arms were

folded across his belly, which was heaving up and down with rage. His cheeks were bright red. With each breath his belly jiggled. He was furious. Smoking mad.

"Oh, my gosh, Willie," my sister whispered.

Lila ran away. She scuttled down the hallway into Mom's bedroom as fast as her legs could carry her, dragging Chicken Bones with her.

I was running right behind her. I wasn't going to stick around. I dashed after my sister and slammed the door behind us and leaned my back against it. "Holy mackerel," I gasped. "It's Santa Claus!"

Lila and Chicken Bones were two quivering lumps under the covers of Mom's bed. "Is he going to kill us?" her muffled voice came out.

"I just hope he starts with you. You got him wicked angry."

"It's your fault, Willie!"

"It is not! I can't believe you told Santa he stinks."

"You called Santa a liar, Willie! You said he was a fat idiot!" She started crying under the covers. "Boo-hoo-hoo! Baw!"

"Maybe we can get out a window." I crossed the little

Lila's sobbing had begun to throttle back. "Uh-uh-uh—is he still there, Willie?"

"How do I know?"

"Go look."

"Go look yourself."

"No!" She started sobbing again. "Baw hoo hoo! Santa Claus hates us, Willie!"

I listened intently at the door. "He probably just gave up on us."

Her sobs stopped instantly. "Oh, no, I hope not."

"What, are you crazy? We need to get him out of here."

"He's Santa, Willie!"

"It's just some dumb ghost faking it," I said, not very convincingly. "Let's go look, okay?"

Lila folded her hands. "Mr. Santa?"

"Yeah?"

"Try some of Willie's cocoa. I love cocoa, 'specially in a blizzard."

He touched his mug, then shook his hand.

"Careful, it's hot," I said.

"How come you're grumpy, Mr. Santa?" Lila asked.

"Because there's not many kids who truly believe in me anymore. It would make you grumpy, too."

"I believe in you," Lila said.

"Your brother doesn't."

"Yeah, I do."

"Uh-uh, Santa. Willie said I was retarded 'cause I believed in you. *Ow!*"

I had kicked her under the table.

The spirit of Santa Claus fixed his stare on me. "Kick your sister again, boy, and you will regret it."

Lila gave me a smirk.

"Did you see that, Santa? She stuck her tongue out at me."

He gave us a stare. "There are two different types of coal. Anthracite coal and bituminous coal. Children like you get to pick."

That shut us up.

Santa blew on his cocoa and took a little slurp of it. It disappeared down his throat—now that was a neat trick, I thought, for a ghost. In the dinette window, the snow was whirling down and piling up against the glass. "The other thing that's got me down," he went on, "is the delivery job every Christmas Eve. It's getting to be a nightmare. Kids wanting more and more stuff." He erupted in a whiny voice: *"'Dear Santa, I want a cherry-red Stingray bicycle with a banana seat, PLUS I want a BB gun so I can kill a whole load of frogs.' 'Dear Santa, You better not forget to bring me those skis I asked for plus that ski trip to Colorado OR ELSE.' 'Dear Santa, I want two Barbies plus I want a Ken doll even if Ken is a dork, and plus do NOT forget to bring me the electric Easy-Bake Oven with all the different mixes, PLUS—.'"* He sighed and ran his hand over his crew cut. "It seems as if nobody cares about the important things."

"Like what?" I asked.

He put down his mug and laid his great hands on the table. "Like giving when you have nothing left to give, boy." He scratched the curly white hair on his chest, which poked up through the neck of his shirt. His suspenders were bright red: why hadn't I noticed that before?

"How did you turn into a ghost, Santa?" my sister asked.

"I'm not a ghost, I'm a spirit. And this is not for children's ears."

That drove my sister crazy. She started bouncing up and down. "That's not fair, Santa! You have to tell us!"

He sighed.

"Please? I'll be *sooo* good if you tell us how you turned into a ghost. Please? I promise."

"Well—" He sipped his hot chocolate. "It happened last Christmas Eve. Right at the end of the night. I crashed."

"Was it bad?" Lila asked fearfully.

"Fearsome. I was wiped out in the crash, lost my sleigh and everything. Perhaps I had a bit too much ale before I took off—it is cold and lonely riding on the wind, and my elves do make a tasty Christmas ale—but let me tell you, flying is magnificent. That is what made it good, the flying. And sometimes I gave an astonishing present to some poor lad or lass who had not asked for it and never expected it, and that was a great satisfaction. I liked to follow the rivers. I wonder if you know that about me: I follow the rivers. It is something to follow a river. I would spy a great, winding river, and I would take the reindeer down low and fast, swinging back and forth, following the bends like this—" His hand swooped and swayed over the dinette table as we listened to his story, our eyes wide. "Following a river," he said, "is like . . . is like—a dream. The reindeer loved it.

"Well, I forgot about something. I forgot about the Hoover Dam. We smacked into the Hoover Dam! People were thrown out of their beds for miles around! It's just a lucky thing the dam didn't burst and drown everybody afterward. It happened so fast I never felt a thing. There was nothing left of my sleigh but a scorch mark on the cement. The only thing that survived the accident was my wrecking bar."

"For trailers?" Lila asked, wide-eyed.

"Yeah, the one I use for getting into trailers. Some kids found it lying at the bottom of the dam. They thought it was a giant peppermint candy cane, and they ate it. It was all burned and greasy, and it gave 'em the runs."

"That's nasty, Santa," Lila said.

"Yeah. But you have to be a real moron to mistake a peppermint wrecking bar for a candy cane."

A scared look crossed Lila's face. "What about . . . the reindeers?"

"They didn't suffer, and that was a blessing."

Lila started whimpering.

"Hey, now—"

She burst into tears.

"Hey, stop that—"

"Your reindeers are dead!" she wailed. "You're a ghost! Your sleigh got burned up! You lost all your presents! You can't bring us any presents this Christmas!" she sobbed.

"That is true. I was wiped out."

Lila would not stop crying.

I glared at her. "Go play on your bunk, brat."

Sniffling and hiccuping, Lila slid out of the dinette nook. She picked up her baby seal and climbed onto her bunk.

"Quit staring at us," I said to her. To him I said in a low voice: "Look, Santa, we need to talk. Outside."

He gave me a strange look, but he unsqueezed himself from the dinette nook. I put on my coat and held the door open for him, and he lumbered down our snowy steps into the wind. We stood in the snow. It was getting dark, and the wind was blasting. The *Sarah Ann* stood in blurry silhouette before us. I shouted, "What's wrong with you?"

He just stared at me.

"Look, you have to give my sister *something* for Christmas. Even if it's just a toothbrush or something," I said over the wind. "Look, I can buy a toothbrush for you at Reilly's Market. But you have to give it to her."

The ghost of Santa just kept on staring at me. I could hardly bear it when he stared at me that way.

"Don't you understand?" I went on. "She's a little girl, and she's just lost her dad. She doesn't really understand about . . . you know . . . death. We don't even know what happened to him. There was nothing left of him. Lila's my little sister, and I have to take care of her now. I will always take care of Lila, no matter what comes. She's my little sister . . . but it's not the same as . . . not the same . . . not the same as having . . ." I went back

"That's pretty," she said in a small voice.

"I see a dollhouse. It is a great giant dollhouse, with lace canopy beds with little colored quilts on them, and it has fireplaces and staircases and chairs and tables and teacups and perfect tiny silver. I'm dreaming of a puppy—huh?"

She whispered something in his ear.

"It's a Jack Russell. His name? Uh—it's Jack. He's a barky little fellow who wants everybody to think he's so big, but he's just a baby, and when he's tired he has to curl up with you. . . . How am I doing?" He opened his eyes and looked at her. His eyes were startlingly blue.

"Pretty good," Lila said.

"You will understand, young lady, that these are your dreams. I cannot give them to you because they already belong to you, my dear."

My sister didn't get it. She seemed to think she was going to get everything Santa was talking about. An uncomfortable look crept over his puffy old face. I think he was beginning to realize that my sister's dreams were headed for a train wreck on Christmas morning.

He turned briskly to me. "What about you, boy?"

"What about me?"

"Did you want to try this?"

"Yeah." I walked over to him.

"Don't speak." He closed his eyes.

I bent over his ear. His cheek was covered with tiny burst blood vessels. A tuft of hair poked out of his ear. I said into his ear, and not softly, "You can cut out the professional act, Santa. All I want is my dad back."

The spirit of Nicholas Dexter Claus looked up at me with shocked eyes. His face went all beefy and red. "I can't help you with that, boy." He lurched to his feet and was gone.

Lila had a cow. "You scared Santa away! I hate you!" She got inside her sleeping bag, and her muffled sobs took a long time to quiet down.

There was thumping on the steps, and Mom opened the door, and a burst of snow came into the trailer with her. She was home from work, and she had walked up the driveway. "Are you okay?" she said, and she put a bag of groceries on the table.

"Santa Claus was here!" Lila said, sitting up in her sleeping bag. "He talked to us! Willie made him hot chocolate! He's going to bring us presents!"

"He'll do his best. He's had a hard time this year."

"I know! He crashed into the Hoover Dam! His sleigh got all burned up and some kids ate his wrecking bar and they got the poopies and he lost all his presents and it was really really bad, Mommy!"

Mom looked weirded out. "Santa will do his best even if he can't bring you everything you want."

***

The storm ended on the morning before Christmas Eve. Mom had to work a half day at the supermarket. We were buried in snow. Mom walked down the driveway to her car, and, soon afterward, the spirit of Nicholas Dexter Claus appeared, sitting in the recliner and watching television.

"I was hoping we got rid of you," I said.

"It's not easy to get rid of me, boy."

"You're going to bring all the presents at Christmas, aren't you, Santa?" Lila broke in.

He didn't answer her, he just touched a haze of white stubble on his cheeks, for his beard was beginning to come back. "I've been thinking about the others."

"What others?" I said.

"Boy, it's Christmas Eve tonight."

"So what else is new."

"There's no reason we can't bring some dreams to people who need them, but I will need your help to do this."

We didn't understand what he meant. He got up and opened the door of the trailer, went down the steps, and began to make his way across the meadow, wading slowly through the deep snow. The wind had shifted to the west, and the clouds were breaking apart and scudding over the land. The sun was shining in patches over the sea, and the trees on the islands were frosted like sugar candy. The sea was bright and dark and beating with a slow swell. "Say, boy, is there a shovel around here?"

I found the snow shovel buried against the trailer. I started after him, walking in his footsteps and carrying the shovel. Lila followed after me, walking in our steps.

The truck was buried, and the *Sarah Ann* was covered with snow. He climbed up on the flatbed trailer and stared up at the boat.

I got up next to him. "That's my dad's boat," I said.

"Give me ten fingers, boy."

I took off my mittens and locked my fingers together. He stepped on my hands, and I boosted him up into Dad's boat. To my surprise, Santa Claus was as light as a feather. I wondered how he had made our trailer shake. I handed the shovel up to him, and he began shoveling snow out of the boat, grunting with effort.

Lila watched. "What are you doing, Santa?"

A burst of snow flew out of the boat. "Getting . . . ready . . . for . . . Christmas . . . Eve," came his voice with each burst of snow. Then we heard a *whump*: he'd thrown back the cover of the engine box. Then we heard: "Oh, *no*. There's a Studebaker engine in here." He came over to the side and looked down at us. "This flew open, and Lila came running out holding something in her fingers. "Look! My tooth fell out!"

The lobstermen grinned, and Mom caught her up and hushed her, and told her that these were Dad's friends who had done a great thing.

"We miss Will Foster more than we can say," Brian Hanscom said from the middle of the group. "So we don't say it."

Mr. Thacker, meanwhile, ordered the truck driver to let the *Sarah Ann* be set down in the meadow. "Who cut this chain?" he said. Then he sat in his car to finish counting his money.

The fishermen of New Harbor gathered together and passed away down our driveway, with Captain Edward Flint leading the way. He was a small, hard man whom the ocean would claim just two years later, when the *Break of Day* lost power in the waters east of Port Clyde, and he was swept to his death onto the Roaring Bull.

encouraged his reindeer, and we soared over Monhegan Island, letting out dreams the whole way. Lila started to shiver, so he told me to go down in the cuddy cabin and get her a blanket. Then Lila stood beside me wrapped in Dad's blanket, holding Chicken Bones, her eyes shining and her hair whipping in the wind, while the deer pulled in perfect unison, their bodies surging, their breath coming in smoky gasps. The stars up there were like diamonds.

He might not have been much of a seaman, but Santa Claus did know how to fly a lobster boat. We went over Matinicus Island, and over Beal's Island, and we did the rest of the Maine coast, letting out dreams the whole way, and I saw the Bay of Fundy in the distance. Then Santa said we had to turn around and go the other way to follow the night, because we had a world to cover with dreams before dawn.

We swung south by west and crossed Massachusetts, trailing dreams. We crossed New York and Ohio, and over Indiana he told the deer they were lazy, mangy, flea-bitten, spavined wretches and he'd feed them nothing but old hay and no sugar if they didn't stop fooling around. The deer responded by doubling their speed, and I swear we laid a sonic boom as we crossed Chicago. Meanwhile I was watching the dream dial. It was going down fast. Too fast. "You aren't planning to do China, are you?" I shouted. "There isn't enough dream-stuff in here."

He didn't answer.

"I hate to break the news, Santa, but they don't have Christmas in Japan and China," I said. "And what about the Moslems and the Jews? A lot of them aren't even Christians, I don't think."

He whirled around and pointed his finger at me. "Every person is entitled to a dream, and every person gets one. Now give your sister a turn."

"She'll mess it up—"

"That's enough, boy!"

I was right, of course. "Whee!" my sister yelled, and she cranked the dream valve wide open, and there was a *whing-bang-buuuoinng* sound, and a wicked hiss, and a clank, and the needle on the dream gauge went down to zero.

Santa's eyes went all wide. "Good heavens, Lila. I

think you just gave three billion dreams to one person down there."

"You killed somebody!" I yelled at her. I turned to Santa. "I told you—"

He cut me off. "DREAMS HURT NO ONE. THE PERSON WHO RECEIVED THREE BILLION DREAMS SURELY DESERVED THEM ALL, AND IF YOU DON'T STOP TALKING BACK TO ME, BOY, I SHALL THROW YOU OVER THE SIDE."

I thought it would be advisable not to answer Santa Claus immediately. He was turning out to be a little unpredictable. I gave him some time to work his blood pressure down, and then I said, "So what's your plan now?" He was spinning the Studebaker steering wheel as if nothing had happened.

He didn't answer. It started to make me nervous.

"We will give what we have." He leaned over the side, and he began to speak. His voice was very loud:

"Can you hear me down there? Whether you are awake or asleep, I give you my dreams. I am dreaming now . . . dreaming of wonders. I am dreaming you got a Lionel train set with a Hudson steam engine that puffs out real smoke and has all the most popular railroad cars including the rocket-launcher car and the exploding boxcar!" He yelled this into the wind, holding his Santa hat on his head with one hand. "I'm dreaming you got a horse, a beautiful roan mare, and you rode her up on the levee and galloped for miles! I'm dreaming you got a Ted Williams autographed baseball bat!" He coughed and spat over the side, and kept going. "I'm dreaming you got all the records of the Beatles, and you got a record player to play them on. A stereo record player . . ." He steadied himself on the wheel house.

"Where was I?" he went on. "I'm dreaming that the wars all over the Earth stopped! I'm dreaming of forgiveness, and I'm dreaming of perfect moves. I see a dancer in my mind's eye, and she is dancing before us in perfect grace, yet she is so lost in her dance that she forgets we are watching! I am dreaming of your dreams!" he shouted. "You can be incredible! You can even be yourself! I am dreaming of your lives, children, and I am dreaming of greatness. I see the yellow and gold leaves of trees falling gently down on the river as the river carries them away, and I'm dreaming of the look in your lover's eyes as he turned to you that day by the river and said he was yours to the end of time! I'm dreaming they put down their guns all over the Earth! I dreamed that all the killing stopped, and afterward I heard the sound of voices telling wonderful stories! I'm dreaming someone paid off your credit card for you! I'm dreaming you learned passable French! I'm dreaming you wanted to be a poet, so you wrote a poem that was actually published in the newspaper. Only one person read your poem, a person who was thinking of suicide, but your poem saved that person's life! I'm dreaming you baked a perfect chocolate cake! I dreamed the Red Sox won the World Series!"

"Now he's lost his wing nut," I remarked to Lila.

He looked back at us. "I can't do this by myself."

Lila went up front and stood next to him by the steering wheel, and looked over the gunwale. "I'm scared, Santa. It's so far."

"Hold my hand. I will not let you fall."

She started dreaming. "Hi, everybody, it's me, Lila Foster!" she yelled over the side. "I dreamed you got a supergiant lollipop! I dreamed you got the world's giantest bear hug! I dreamed you got a little baby kitten!"

"Nice," he said. Then he looked at me. "Boy, you are needed."

"This is kind of dumb," I said.

He glared at me, and shouted over the side: "I dreamed that, in fact, you did learn to fly by flapping your arms! I dreamed you learned to speak the silent language of trees! I dreamed you walked the immortal beach at the end of time! I dreamed you found the last digit of pi! I dreamed you got enough to eat! I dreamed that all the beatings stopped! I dreamed the torturers forgot their art!"

Lila leaned out. "I dreamed your stocking got so full it went *kaboom!* I dreamed you had a friend like Chicken Bones!"

"I'm waiting, boy."

Finally I stood next to my sister. "Well, you got a new car."

"That's pathetic."

"Well, it's a Mustang," I said to him.

"Don't say it to me, boy. Say it over the side."

"You got a Mustang!" I said over the side.

"How about some detail?"

"It's a red Mustang! It's a convertible! It's turbocharged! It has street-legal slicks! It has a girlfriend in it!" I shouted over the side.

"We're getting there," he muttered. He took a breath and shouted, "I dreamed that in spite of your autism you had dear friends!"

"I dreamed your lost dog came home!" Lila yelled.

"I dreamed you broke the world record ski jump at the Olympics," I said.

"Improvement," he said.

"I dreamed you were an astronaut! I dreamed you landed on Mars!" I yelled.

He hung over the side and boomed: "I have a dream, that all God's children—black, white, red, yellow, and every other amazing color—are walking together in the rain and in the dust and in the hot sun, and they are helping one another down the long road wherever it goes. I dreamed you were hit by a car, and it was a wondrous piece of luck, because when you were lying on the pavement and dying in pain, it occurred to you that you were alive!"

"I dreamed you found an ice-cream cone that changes flavors and is never used up and is just a little goopy!"

"I dreamed my sister was never sad," I said.

A warmth fell on my shoulder; it was his hand.

"I dreamed Willie got a girlfriend," Lila said, and stuck her tongue out at me.

I yelled, "I dreamed you became a rock star! I dreamed you found the most valuable treasure on Earth!"

"And the treasure you found," Santa shouted, "was the Earth. I'm dreaming of red-tailed hawks, the way they stream south along the ridges! I'm dreaming of sequoia trees, thrusting their ancient spires at the moon! I'm dreaming of canyons, deepening imperceptibly with every droplet of rain! I'm dreaming of whales, the way they breach and throw the sea off their backs! I'm dreaming of prairies, ignited with flowers from horizon to horizon! For twelve billion years I have dreamed! Such a long time to dream, yet it was no time at all! I dreamed that time did not register its flow! I dreamed that what registered in the end was only love, for love is the only power strong enough to shake time to its core and make it loosen its grip! What is wrong with you people? Have you forgotten how to love?"

He seemed to be working himself into a passion. He

suddenly tore off his fake beard and threw it over the side; then he hung on to the winch arm and leaned out dangerously far. His voice really started booming now. "Where is the love I put in your hearts? What are you doing with it? Did you lose it somewhere? Did you stuff your love into a paper bag like a half-eaten sandwich, and leave it somewhere on a park bench? Do you understand the power of the love I have given you? Are you blind? Do you not see the mountains thrown down and the sea raised to the sky? Do you not see my power and my mercy? I almost drowned you, have you forgotten that? And then I gave you a rainbow! And then I gave you all I had."

Lila and I squinched down in the stern.

"Santa's getting grumpy. I think he needs to go to bed," she whispered.

"Why do you break my heart?" he roared in a voice that seemed to roll like a tidal wave across the world. "Why do I still love you so? What makes you think you are so special? Don't you know I made the sharks in my image, too? Haven't you heard of my inordinate fondness for beetles?"

Meanwhile he was moving the wheel this way and that, and working the deer. We crossed the Missouri River as he continued to speak. And then he dove the *Sarah Ann* close to the river. We began to follow the Missouri north by west, running over gray and silver waters and over stretches of ice. Santa was silent for a while, mesmerized. We followed the river up through the Gates of the Rockies, and we climbed into Canada, and then he took us north on a great circle across Alaska. We passed the Aleutian Islands and Japan, and we did a quick one over Australia, and a slow pass over China and India, and we did Russia and the Middle East, and all the time we took turns dreaming as best we could. Then we came to Africa. Lila was dreaming over the side of the boat, when all of a sudden Chicken Bones slipped out of her hands. We saw him falling, a white speck turning around and around.

"Chicken Bones!" she wailed.

"Follow that seal!" he called to the reindeer. The deer braked and banked, and we rolled and then fell sideways, plummeting like a stone. I thought we would be killed, but he pulled up and landed the *Sarah Ann* in a

desert. Mountains stood around us in the moonlight. There was one dead tree, and there were some huts made of mud and thatch. And there was a little girl standing before a hut, holding Chicken Bones and staring at us. I don't think she had ever seen a lobster boat or reindeer. Chicken Bones must have bounced off her hut and woken her up.

"Where are we?" I asked him.

"Afar," he answered.

That sounded about right to me.

"Can I have my seal back?" Lila said.

The kid just stared at us. She was holding Chicken Bones tight against her tummy, just the way Lila did.

The reindeer were pawing and stamping.

Lila looked to Dexter for help. He shrugged.

My sister spent a long moment thinking. I don't know how she did it, but she said, "His name is Chicken Bones. Please take care of him, okay?"

"Melkam Yelidet Beaal!" Dexter shouted, which I guess meant Merry Christmas in those parts, and in a moment we were back in the sky.

Somewhere over Tierra del Fuego he said we were

done. We had covered the Earth with dreams, he said, and if we had missed any spots, it was no matter, the winds would deliver them there. By then, Lila had fallen asleep in the cuddy berth, wrapped in Dad's blanket. He opened the engine cover and did something to the Lark engine, and there was a ripping sound, and I don't know what happened, but all of a sudden we were in outer space, and the Earth was hanging in front of us, a ball of white and blue. The reindeer were playing around us. They had slipped their reins and were running free.

"I get cranky sometimes," he said, hanging on to the Studebaker wheel with one hand and looking at the Earth. "Well, I've made worse worlds, anyway. Better ones, too." He scratched the white hair of his chest with his great workingman's hand. "Boy," his voice came.

"Here I am." I stood right at attention in the stern. I wanted to look very sharp for him.

"Apparently you have guessed Who I am."

"I think so, Sir."

"You think so."

There was an awkward silence. Finally, I said, not

looking directly at him: "As long as you're here, well—uh—there's a few questions I want to ask you."

There was another awkward silence. "I am not in the habit of answering questions."

"But, well, I did help you."

He sighed. "All right. One question."

"And you'll answer true?"

There was a dangerous growl, and I remembered he said he never lies. Then I started racking my brain. The truth is I had no idea what I wanted to ask him. There were too many questions, and none of them seemed quite right. Finally, I blurted, "Why is there so much pain?"

There was not a sound from him.

I've stumped him, I thought.

No word in reply.

"You didn't answer my question."

He was standing at the wheel with his back to me, and we were looking at the Earth. He spun the wheel, and the *Sarah Ann* came around, and a great shining curtain of stars rolled into view, and it was the Milky Way. There were so many stars out there that they looked like a burning mist of jewels on fire, spreading in oceans across the sky, and the earth was only a speck of dust drifting in the wonder of it all. "Because you are alive," he said in a quiet voice.

"But it doesn't answer my—"

"That's enough! You've been arguing with me, boy, ever since I showed up in your trailer."

Right then, almost too late, I realized there was something very important I needed to ask. "Wait! My sister should get a question. To be fair."

"All right. Make it quick."

I hurried down into the cuddy, where I found Lila curled up in Dad's blanket and sound asleep. "Wake up!" I shook her. "You gotta talk to Dexter. You have to ask him what happened to Dad."

"Ohhh . . . Willie—"

"Get up!" I practically dragged her on deck. She stood before him, shivering in the blanket, half asleep, and I had to hold her upright.

He wasn't even looking at us. He kept his back to us, with one hand on the steering wheel, and he was still looking at the Earth and the stars beyond.

"Dexter? My sister has a question for you."

"Go ahead," came his voice.

I whispered to Lila: "Ask him what happened to Dad. Don't mess up."

"Santa?" my sister said drowsily.

"I am listening."

"If you're dead and you're a ghost, does that mean you can't ever bring us any more presents ever again?"

"What a stupid ques—"

I was cut off by a gentle laugh, and he said over his shoulder, "Young lady, where did you get the idea that I am a ghost? I never said I was a ghost. I am a spirit. I never said I was dead, either. When I hit the Hoover Dam, I never felt a thing. I lost my sleigh. Who cares? It can be replaced, of course, and there will always be presents. I am everywhere in the world with all hearts and all people, and I give out love and dreams at Christmas. I am the spirit of Christmas, and I cannot die."

"That's what I thought," Lila said.

"You did not," I whispered to her. I turned to him and said loudly, "I just want to know what happened to my dad."

Everything got quiet. Time held its breath.

Then something strange happened with him. He had been standing with his back to us while he spoke, and now there seemed to be a glow coming around his head. The glow was lighting up the Studebaker steering wheel and the inside of the wheelhouse. Suddenly he turned around and looked at us, and there was a huge burst of light, and he showed us his face. The real face.

We had just a glimpse of it. We saw only a part of the face, and only for the briefest moment. We saw the line of the cheekbone coming around. Then the pupil of the eye flicked toward us, and he was looking at us.

It was not the face of a man. It seemed to me more like a woman. Yet it was not a woman, either, or a child. It had all of us in it. And the light of the face was so bright, and it hurt so, that I could not bear it. I squeezed my eyes shut and clamped my hands over my eyes. You know how if you hold a flashlight against your hands in the dark you can see a glow coming through your hands? The light went through the flesh of my hands, and even then it was so bright that if you'd looked straight into the sun in that light pouring through my hands, the sun would have seemed like a spot of the blackest soot. I could feel the light hammering at my bones and tugging at my body like an undertow.

"You won't set the boat on fire, will you, Sir? It's my dad's boat."

There was a chuckle, and the light dimmed.

He had given his answer about Dad, though not with words. It has taken me years to understand what he meant, and though I will never understand it completely, I think I know what the light was made of. It was the only power that is strong enough to sweep time away. Even as the light faded I could feel it was there and would always be there. But I still could not look at the face, so I looked at the seas of stars all around, and I didn't know what to say. Finally, I said, "You did a nice job making the universe, Sir."

He snorted. "It's just a cobbled rig to hold the dreams."

"You have a nice face, Santa," my sister suddenly said. That was when I realized she had not closed her eyes.

"You need to get some rest, young lady. Why don't you let your brother tuck you in?"

"Good night, Santa."

"You be good to your brother. He loves you very much, you know."

She already had her thumb in her mouth. I carried her back down into the cuddy and got the blanket all snug around her in Dad's berth, and kissed her on the forehead. I went back up on deck. I was extremely nervous about what might happen next. I did not want to be alone with Dexter.

But when I got back up on deck, fortunately he was back to his old self, the fat man in the red suit. That was a relief.

I sat down on the stern.

He gave a great sigh. "Stern man."

"Did you mean me, Sir?"

"Yes, you. Tell me a joke."

"What?" It took me by surprise.

"All they do is talk about their problems. Don't they know I could use a laugh once in a while?"

I had to think fast. "Okay . . . uh . . . how do you tell the difference between boogers and broccoli?"

"Hold on! I said no more questions."

"It's not a question, Sir. It's a riddle."

"Oh—a riddle." He scratched his crew cut, and the boat wallowed. "What are you doing asking me riddles? I'm the one who—"

"You don't have to figure it out. You just say, 'I don't know, what is the difference?'"

"All right, all right," he said testily. "What is the difference between boogers and broccoli?"

"Kids won't eat broccoli."

He grinned. He grabbed his stomach "Ha! Ha! Where did you hear that? HAW! HAW! Get the steering wheel—"

I assumed the helm.

He staggered past me, clutching his belly. "HO! HO! HO!" He rang it out all over the world, HO! HO! HO! MERRY CHRISTMAS!"

It was the loudest laugh I had ever heard, and his stomach did shake like a bowl full of jelly. He laughed for a while, and then he sat down on the stern deck. "Whoof . . . you nearly busted my gut. You are a piece of work, stern man. All right, take her down east."

My heart swam. Take her down east. For there is something about turning the helm of a fine old wooden boat downwind and toward the east that goes beyond words. I moved the wheel gently, and the *Sarah Ann* leaped at my touch.

He sat on the stern watching me steer. Then he slapped the stern deck. "Not a bad boat."

"Built by the Swetts of Friendship, Sir. Their last boat."

"It's a good one."

We landed beside our trailer in a cloud of smoke from the Lark just as the sun was breaking. He pulled off his red suit and hung it on the slicker peg. Underneath he was still wearing his work clothes, looking every inch a lobster fisherman. He started to heave himself over the side, but he paused. Something was on his mind. "Say, Will. I guess you understand that I could not bring your father back."

"I know that. I'll be all right."

"Oh, I'm not worried about you. But I wanted to say there was no need to bring him back. It was your mother's love for him that saved his life." There was a ripple in the world, and Dexter was gone. I carried my sister into the trailer.

On Christmas Day we opened a few small presents. Lila opened mine, the stuffed monkey. "It's Hubert-Don't-Ask-Me-Why!" she yelled and hugged him. "I just love him!"

Not long after that, our telephone rang. It was a doctor calling from Da Nang Hospital in Vietnam. He informed us that Dad was in the unit there. He had been shot in the chest, and his dog tags had been clipped off by the bullet. A patrol had found him in the mud, unconscious but breathing. The infection that developed in his wound afterward was so bad that he forgot his name, and nobody knew who he was, and the doctors almost gave up on him. They said he kept calling, "Sarah Ann. Sarah Ann." He did not mean the boat. That was how they finally learned his name, by tracing hers. I guess I should have said at the beginning that this is a love story.

It was a raw day in March when he came home. At first we heard his voice singing. He was coming up the driveway, singing, "I think we're alone now / The beating of our hearts is the only sound . . ." His voice was as bad as ever.

We practically destroyed the Crashmaster getting out the door to see him. There he was, walking slowly along the stone wall under the white pine trees, carrying a duffel bag over his shoulder—my father, William T. Foster Sr., considerably thinner but as tall and handsome and true as ever a man was made.

He dropped his bag and caught Mom and me and Lila at the same time. We nearly knocked him to the ground, but he held his feet, and I felt his love come around us, folding our family with peace and keeping us safe forever.

That was when I knew, with the clearness of simple truth, that our dreams are real. A stern man is not in a position to offer guarantees, but I believe we can somehow find our way in the end. I believe we must hold on to our dreams and never let them go, for I think the cobbled rig he spoke of was meant to be filled with our dreams. And when a dream seems impossible, that means it has at least a chance. This is in spite of the fact that I do not believe the Red Sox will win the World Series any time soon.

Dad said to me, "You've grown a lot. I think you can be my stern man once in a while this summer. And you know, when I was in the hospital, I had this funny dream I was making your sister a boat. A little white rowboat with blue oars. Want to build it with me?"

For their expertise and help, special thanks to
  Greg Rössel
  Ben Ellison
  Rich Hilsinger